FUN ON THE JOB

AMUSING AND TRUE TALES FROM
ROSIE-THE-RIVETERS TO ROCKET SCIENTISTS AT A
MAJOR AEROSPACE COMPANY

FUN ON THE JOB:
AMUSING AND TRUE TALES FROM
ROSIE-THE-RIVETERS TO ROCKET SCIENTISTS AT A
MAJOR AEROSPACE COMPANY

*to Linda Vista library
fans & readers — Here are
tales That many Linda Vistans
can relate to and were a
part of.   Tom Leech
                      San Diego
                      author*

TOM LEECH

**Presentations
Press**

FUN ON THE JOB: Amusing and true tales from Rosie-the-Riveters to Rocket Scientists at a major aerospace company

Presentations Press, San Diego, CA, USA

Library of Congress Control Number: 2017931278

ISBN-13: 978-0981769332 (Presentations Press)

ISBN-10: 0981769330

Website: presentationspress.com

5694 Mission Center Road., #602-329, San Diego, CA 92108

858-650-0810

email tomaseb@aol.com

Books can be ordered at amazon.com, presentationspress.com, and (wholesale) at Ingram.

"This documentation of the transition from rivets to rockets at General Dynamics provides insight into the diversity of employees' personalities and technical skills. The reader will probably find comparable examples of their own work experience at the other aerospace companies. A comfortable way to remember the good old days." — **C. K. Anderson, Director at Convair, Data Systems and Electronics Divisions**

"Thousands of people spent millions of man-hours developing the Atlas. But not all of those hours were spent on space business—many were spent on funny business. People, being ordinary people, often had time on their hands. We Rickety Rocketeers at Cape Canaveral had lots of idle time between launches and we engaged in a lot of "Funny business." Tom Leech has collected many stories of our mischief during those idle hours and provided them to you in this book. Read them and you will see that we were not all "Steely eyed rocket scientists." — **Leroy Gross, Head Rickety Rocketeer**

"Building rocket weapons of mass destruction was serious business. Turning those rockets into <u>peaceful</u> explorers of the universe was another thing. Behind each were extraordinary humans, with interesting stories to tell, presented in this book compiled by Tom Leech, who was there." — **Bill Ketchum, Propulsion Engineer on many programs**

TOM LEECH

BOOKS BY TOM LEECH

(A VERSATILE AUTHOR)

SAY IT LIKE SHAKESPEARE:
THE BARD'S TIMELESS TIPS FOR COMMUNICATION SUCCESS

Second Edition. Presentations Press 2013 (Previously published in 2001 by McGraw-Hill with subtitle *How to Give a Speech like Hamlet, Persuade like Henry V, and other Secrets from the World's Greatest Communicator*)

THE CURIOUS ADVENTURES OF SANTA'S WAYWARD ELVES

with Leslie Johnson-Leech, Presentations Press 2014

ON THE ROAD IN '68:
A YEAR OF TURMOIL, A JOURNEY OF FRIENDSHIP

Presentations Press 2009.

OUTDOORS SAN DIEGO:
HIKING, BIKING AND CAMPING

with Jack Farnan, Premier 2004

HOW TO PREPARE, STAGE & DELIVER WINNING PRESENTATIONS

Third Edition, AMACOM American Management Association 2004

CONTENTS

ACKNOWLEDGEMENTS

I worked for the General Dynamics (GD) San Diego Astro-Convair operations from 1959-1980, with some leave getaways along the way. In this set of amusing tales, you'll hear from many colleagues I knew during my years there, and many with their stories way before and long after my specific time. Thanks to all the past (and some still current) GD troops who have sent me their tales and made encouraging comments about the idea of a book combining the stories. This is that result.

We started this project around 2011, with e-mails the main communication method, though several contributors from earlier years are not computer fans so they sent in their stories mostly hand-written. Since starting the project, several of the contributors have passed on, adding to the priority of getting these tales out there.

Also, several GD cronies have helped me push this project along, with suggestions, content review, and actual book concept. Thanks to Jack Smothers, Burt Brockett, Bill Vega, Chuck DeMund and Keith Anderson. And thanks for editorial help from Patsy Powell Corlett and significantly from Rick Lakin of iCrew Digital Publishing.

Finally I dedicate this book to two very special people from my life. My father, John Earl Leech, and my mother, Catherine Leech, provided me and my siblings with a growing-up life filled with love, enjoyment, and inspiration, They are both long-departed but a constant source of special memories.

CHAPTER 1—OVERVIEW

Who hasn't spent some time on their job, whatever it has been, to have experienced a few amusing activities while doing that assignment? The idea behind this book is to assemble a whole bunch of those, given this one operation had decades of jobs done by thousands of employed folks for one major U.S. company, General Dynamics (GD) and its predecessor companies. The many amusing stories here come from many tasks, products and locations.

The idea was for contributors to send their personal memories of the humorous stories from their experience working for GD, whether at San Diego, launch sites or anywhere. As many events are ongoing where vets gather with past cronies for weekly, monthly and annual gatherings, the tales fly back and forth.

A BRIEF HISTORY OF GENERAL DYNAMICS

This company started its San Diego life in 1935, when Reuben Fleet moved his company there, from Buffalo, New York. Known as Consolidated Aircraft Company, it quickly became a major force providing aircraft for the United States Army and Navy. Many PBY amphibian aircraft were built during the late 1930s.

Fleet sold the company in 1940 and later it took on the name Consolidated-Vultee. Consolidated's B-24 Liberator bomber was a major force in World War II and by war's end, more B-24's had been produced than any four-engine aircraft in history. With so many men called to the fight, many women were brought into the work force. It was not easy for the enemy to spot the company as the major assembly plant near downtown San Diego was covered over with a huge cloth.

By the close of World War II, Consolidated-Vultee became Convair. By the close of the war, Convair employment took a major hit, dropping from a wartime peak of 43,000 to just 3,000 workers. The company made a major shift from military bombers to commercial passenger liners, with the propeller-driven 240 and 440 twin-engine Convair Liners gaining major shares of the airline market. Convair entered the Jet Age with experimental delta-winged XF-92 aircraft and production of the F-102 and F-106 delta-wing fighters. Convair entered the competitive 4-engine large passenger jetliner game with the 880 and 990, though financial success was not easy, and major layoffs occurred in the mid-sixties.

Convair was merged into General Dynamics in 1954. In the late fifties, GD set up a new Astronautics division and totally new facility at San Diego's mostly barren Kearny Mesa. The initial product was the liquid-fueled Atlas ICBM (Intercontinental Ballistic Missile), which became a major factor in US-Soviet Cold War relations. Atlas took on a different role as the booster rocket for the final four manned Mercury missions beginning in February, 1962 when Col. John H. Glenn, USMC, became the first American to orbit the Earth. The weapon and space programs led to operations at military activation bases nationwide, plus launch operations at Cape Kennedy in Florida and Vandenberg Air Force Base in California. Atlas and the Centaur upper stage continue to be major forces in U.S. space pursuits.

The Astronautics name disappeared in the late sixties when San Diego operations combined under the continuing name Convair. In 1985 the Atlas and Centaur operations became a new GD Space Systems Division.

A major new product, the Cruise Missile, to be fired from submarines, appeared in the seventies. Following major competitions, Convair won the contract and the weapon took on the name Tomahawk. It proved a successful weapon launched from multiple naval, aircraft, and ground systems. Later GD sold that operation and the Tomahawk Missile continues to be a key force in U.S. military operations.

In the early eighties, the Air Force deemed it necessary to upgrade their nuclear Air-Launched Cruise Missile (ALCM), with a next generation stealth version. Convair bested the incumbent Air Force contractor, Boeing and the Lockheed Skunk Works, to win this major program. The Advanced Cruise Missile (ACM) was a key in convincing the Soviets to back off the nuclear arms race and eventually the Cold War. Later GD sold the cruise missile operation and while the nuclear ACM was eventually retired, the conventional weapon Tomahawk continues to be a key force.

By the mid 1990s most of the San Diego GD aerospace operations were phased out. The entire huge Kearny Mesa facility was physically eliminated. The Lindbergh Field large plant facilities were gone. The products and many of the key employees have continued at other companies, and locations.

That's a quick summary of most of the major operations and products tied to the San Diego company. You'll hear from many of the people who worked on those products and multiple locations, with the concept…

FUN ON THE JOB: Amusing and true tales from Rosie-the-Riveters to Rocket Scientists at a major aerospace company.

CHAPTER 2—1930-40s

Primary operations at Consolidated and Consolidated Vultee included:

- B-24 Liberator bomber
- PBY Catalina Amphibian
- B-32 Dominator bomber
- Convair-Liner 240 commercial aircraft
- Terrier unpiloted antiaircraft weapon
- MX-774 ballistic missile

FROM SUSAN FLEET WELSCH

Susan is the daughter of Reuben Fleet, yes—founder of Consolidated Aircraft Co., the one he moved from Buffalo, New York, to San Diego in 1935.

SOME REUBEN FLEET TALES

I'm finally getting around to a couple of stories told to me by my half-brother, David G. Fleet, who was 35 years older than I. David worked with our dad, Reuben H. Fleet, long before I was born.

In 1988, while I was clearing out our parents' home in Point Loma after both of my parents had passed away, I came across a photograph of a man I did not recognize. I asked David who this person was, and my brother told me it was John Hertz. David said that Mr. Hertz was on the Board of Directors of Consolidated Aircraft Corporation, our dad's company. Mr. Hertz had founded Yellow Cab Company in Chicago in 1915 and in 1924 had started Hertz Car Rentals.

Count Fleet winning the Kentucky Derby May 1, 1943   Courtesy Wikipedia

My brother said that what was interesting about the Hertz family was that John Hertz's wife, Fannie, was into breeding and racing thoroughbred horses. She decided to name a very unruly colt (that her husband twice had tried unsuccessfully to sell) after our dad because this horse was "frisky," like our dad. She named this horse, Count Fleet. Count Fleet went on to win the Triple Crown of Thoroughbred Racing in 1943.

PLANE VS. DONKEY

Here's another story my brother, David, told me. When dad was in charge of training pilots at North Island during World War One, one of the student pilots hit a donkey after landing on the airfield there. David told me that dad was furious and called the young student pilot to report to him right away.

David said he hid behind the sofa for he knew how angry our dad would be about this incident. David said that when the young man reported in that dad had calmed down by then and told the pilot, "This is a case of one ass hitting another." David had gotten a kick out of that.

ANOTHER TALE ABOUT REUBEN FLEET, A CHAP WHO LOVED TO TALK (ABOUT 1940).

From *Brotherhood of Arms: General Dynamics and the Business of Defending America* by Jacob Goodwin, Published 1985, page 49.

Fleet was an imposing man with a nonstop mouth. Nearly everyone who knew him recalled his fondness for talking. At the drop of an aircraft rivet he would tell the story of his rise in the aviation business, extol the virtues of Consolidated's latest aircraft, or curse the damnable behavior of the Internal Revenue Service.

On one occasion Harry S. Truman, then a senator from Missouri and chairman of the Senate committee investigating the nation's defense program, turned up in San Diego to look over Fleet's aircraft plant. Weary of his host's interminable blather, Truman cut him off. 'God Damn!' Truman interrupted, 'I want to see your books, Fleet! I'm not interested in your rise from rags to riches!'

B-24Ds of 93rd Bomb Group in formation. Nearest aircraft is Joisey Bounce, wingman is The Duchess, and next higher is Bomerang.   Courtesy Wikipedia

FROM PHIL PROPHETT, TEST PILOT, 1940S

A B-24 PILOT'S PRANK???

From *Into the Sunset: The Convair Story* by Bill Yenne, 1995, page 40

"We had an ex-Navy pilot named Bob Baer. One day, he was on a B-24 flight test off-shore when he saw an aircraft carrier. (As a prank) he dropped the landing gear, lowered the flaps, swung around downwind and came into the landing pattern. When he thundered across the flight deck, there wasn't a soul anywhere in sight."

From DORAINE OFFERMAN, Lindbergh Field Tool Room and more

Interesting new hires

I started my career with Convair, on January 16, 1942, as a Department Clerk, in the Tool Room, on the mezzanine of Building Three, Plant Two. When the Navy and local police shut down the "houses of ill repute" south of Market Street, the "girls" all flocked to Consolidated Aircraft. Many of them were hired to work in the Die Shop. All I had to do was look at them and the "voids" on their second sheets, to know their most recent employment! It was a great opportunity, for they could earn a daily wage and make their "nighttime dates!" They were true "double dippers."

In the early forties the guards were extremely fussy about your badge placement. It had to be on your upper chest near the left shoulder. One morning, on the Plant Two overpass, the guards were hassling a cute blond about her badge placement. Her response to the guards was, "I should pin it on my ass, because that is where you are all looking."

Thievery of tools was rampant during the war. At Plant Two the guards would initiate "tool checks!" The first few thieves were caught on the overpass, but the words "tool check" was passed back to the waiting crowd. You could hear the metal hit the concrete as employees divested themselves of their stolen tools. After the crowd had passed, the concrete was a sea of small tools!

A bit lax on the facilities

In 1942 while working in the Tool Room on the mezzanine of Building Three, Plant Two, we girls were all aghast that there was only "one" women's restroom in the middle of the mezzanine. The

Jigs and Fixtures office abutted ours in the far north end of the building.

We girls would band together for the long trek to the restroom. Some wag, down in the Machine Shop, had a whistle on his machine that he would "toot" when we girls started our dash down the gauntlet! The tooting alerted the men below and those on the mezzanine that the girls were coming! The whistles and catcalls were deafening and overrode any machine noise. The men never seemed to tire of this sport and we were beet-red when we reached the restroom. It was then a repeat performance on our return to our offices.

During World War II, ladies nylon stockings were prized possessions!! When the war started, I had quite a supply, but as time went by, my nylons took a beating. The local 54-104 dress store had a nylon mending station and I was a frequent customer! Anything to avoid wearing those "dreaded" rayon stockings! I'm sure that you remember how our GIs used PX nylons to "lure" girlfriends!!

AUTHOR NOTE: The women's restroom issue has a couple relevant events:

- At the GD Astronautics Kearny Mesa facility, the main customer meetings were held in Building Two on the second floor above the circular staircase. And there was only a men's restroom; women attendees had to walk over to one of the other buildings. Then a female military officer/customer noted this was ridiculous and had to change, A female restroom in Building Two swiftly appeared.

- The 2016 movie, "Hidden Figures," was set at NASA in the '50s pre-IBM computer era. Three black women were part of the team as super-math specialists then called Computers. One problem for them was that the nearby restroom was "white only," so they had to walk a long distance for restroom breaks. A high point of the movie is when that problem gets resolved.

From BILL CHANA

From *Over the Wing: the Bill Chana Story*, page 21. Used with permission.

SOMETIMES COMMUNICATION WAS ENTERTAINING

Bill described how early in World War II Consolidated and Boeing received contracts to design new heavy bombers, the Consolidated version called the XB-32. Bill designed and supervised installation of the flight test instrumentation. The first flight was 7 September 1942 with Russ Rogers (see a problem ahead, maybe?) as pilot. Test flights headed out from Lindbergh Field eastward over the Laguna Mountains and desert. On one flight Bill spotted a serious problem with landing doors and described specifics. Then he added this info.

INTERCOM CONFUSION ADDED TO OUR WOES.

An engineering designer by the name of Bob Rogers was on this flight as an observer in the aft cabin. He called the pilot just as we started our climb to return to San Diego. He said "Rogers, this is Rogers, over." Pilot Rogers responded, "Rogers, this is Rogers, what do you have to report? Over." The observer said, "The landing gear doors on number one nacelle are on fire, over." Since there are no landing gear doors on the number one nacelle, those of us listening on the intercom felt that our observer was a little confused and frightened. Pilot Rogers replied, "Rogers, this is Rogers, we know that numbers two and three nacelles have had a fire. We have reduced power on those engines and we are returning to San Diego. Over and out."

As we were beginning our descent after crossing the Laguna Mountain range, Bob Rogers came on the intercom again. "Rogers, this is Rogers. The number one nacelle is still on fire, over!" Russ replied "Rogers, this is Rogers, we have reduced power on all of our engines and will be landing in a few minutes. Keep your eye on the nacelles. Over and out."

It wasn't until we were back on the ground that we discovered how serious the fire had been. The XB-32 had nacelle extension cones attached to the lower surface of the wing flaps. All four nacelle extensions were burned off and the aft sections of all nacelles were charred. The nacelle skins were buckled from the heat. All four main landing gear doors had seen intense fire. Large sections of the outer aluminum skin and inner door frames were missing. The wing flaps themselves were not damaged because the flaps were up for most of the flight.

Lessons to be learned from this flight. One, it would have been wiser to have put the porcelain exhaust deflectors on one inboard nacelle for a flight check. The fire would have been observed, the engine would have been shut-down and this would have left three good engines to come home on. Second lesson, don't go on a test flight with two crew members named Rogers since the word "roger" is used in acknowledging intercom communications.

Note: you may recall a few decades later a movie called "Airplane" came out featuring funny scenes with crew exchanging "Roger, Roger," comments. Did they give Bill Chana appropriate credit?

(This part is not so funny. On May 10, 1943 an XB-32 heading off from Lindbergh Field crashed, killing the pilot and severely burning Bill Chana and two others with another three onboard injured badly. In addition several Marines were injured when the plane crashed through the fence into the Marine Corps Recruit Depot.)

MORE FROM DORAINE

"HANKY-PANKY AMONG THE WORLD WAR TWO WORKFORCE"

(Does this have some sort of familiar ring to it?)

When I worked in the Service Department of Flight and Service (March, 1943 to August, 1944) we had a supervisor who got his "kicks" by putting an arm around the girls, but his hand would go under the arm and squeeze the breast. We soon learned to keep our arms firmly to our sides when we approached when we were approached by "Hands." In those days sexual-harassment was unknown! Female employees were at the mercy of the male employees.

From GD and Aviation Legend, Bill Chana

This item is from his book *Over the Wing: the Bill Chana Story*, page 19, used with family permission.

Getting the Wrong OK Signal

On one planned high-altitude flight in B-24D Number 1 we had an engineering observer on board. This was his first flight in a B-24. Our plan was to go to 30,000 feet. The observer sat in the flight deck gun turret seat. I briefed him on the use of the oxygen regulator and his oxygen mask. I was seated near him. If he thought there was a problem he could tap me on the shoulder.

We started our climb and at 15,000 feet he tapped me on the shoulder and gave me a typical "OK" sign with his thumb and forefinger. At 20,000 feet I got another tap on the shoulder and another "OK" sign. Passing through 25,000 feet the observer slumped in his gun turret chair. Glancing up I could see that he was unconscious.

I immediately called our pilot, Don Scott, and requested a rapid descent. Upon reaching 10,000 feet our friend awakened. I asked him what went wrong. He said "From 15,000 feet and up I was trying to tell you that my oxygen gauge was reading zero." I said "Oh is that what you meant by your hand sign? I thought you meant that everything was OK." Don Scott canceled the flight and returned to Lindbergh Field so that our engineering observer could get a thorough physical examination by the company doctor.

FUN ON THE JOB

FROM DORAINE OFFERMAN

FUN AND GAMES OUT ON THE LINES. ARE YOU SURE YOU'RE READY FOR THESE TALES?

In 1943, I was a Fields Service Inspector in Building Four, Lindbergh Field. Our job was to go thru the B-24, on the Flight Line west of Building Four, to check for the equipment that was required and develop a "shortage list" that went with the aircraft upon delivery to the Air Force. We sometimes had to bike over to Compass Rose to do our final check. The aft of upper wing space was where the oxygen bottles were stored. One lunch time on the flight line, a guard ducked under the open bomb bay doors to check out the airplane. He discovered a couple having sex in the aft of upper wing space. He seemed quite proud of the fact that he had "let them finish" before he nailed them! Unfortunately, they were both married, but not to each other!!

ANOTHER TALE FROM DORAINE

When I worked in Building Three, on the PB2Y3s, it was "rock and roll times" on the lunch hour. The Catalinas had bunks that got a great "workout" before delivery to the Air Force.

BUSINESS AFFAIRS

The secretary to our boss was married to a serviceman who was overseas. She was carrying on an affair with a red-headed service employee. Unfortunately, she wound up pregnant. I transferred to the Tucson Division in August 1944, so I never know how that scenario played out!

One of our service typists was amply endowed and did not wear a brassiere. She was fond of those loose knit sweaters that were popular at the time. This meant that her nipples were on display at times. The typewriter repairman was working on my machine when he happened to look over at the busty typist. His mouth dropped open and he said, quote, "My God, are those real or camouflage!"

Late at night, one of our married supervisors was found out in the middle of the Lindbergh Field runway, drunk as a skunk and with a girlfriend.

During the war, we had a lot of "hijinks" going on. Today's workplace probably has some problems, but people, seemingly, are more discreet.

THOSE LOVELY LADIES ON THE B-24S

Dear Tom, you said that you wanted more of my" Sparky" tales, so here goes!

When I worked, at the Tucson Division, in 1944-1945, we had problems with "sex in the airplanes." We had an Assistant Foreman, on the night shift, who got caught with his pants down!

During early 1944, when I worked in Flight and Service, I and my female coworkers would sit out on the flight line and eat our sack lunches. We would stretch out our bare legs to try and get them tanned while watching the Convair test pilots check out the B-24s before delivery to the Air Force. They did "touch and go" landings. Some of the pilots would come in so low that the B-24 wheels almost touched the fence at Pacific Highway at Laurel Street. We were based in the south Pacific Highway building. This later became part of the Lindbergh Field Airport and then the Weather Station and Jim's Air.

There were times when I got caught up and had a few moments to call my own. I would check out the folders of our Representatives in India and North Africa and read their reports. Our Rep in Australia also had some interesting reports to read. Our handsomest, single Rep was stationed in Natal, Brazil. Unfortunately not much was going on in Natal!

FUN ON THE JOB

Our B-24 crews were famous or infamous, for the names and pictures they painted it on their airplanes. On lunch hour we would venture out to the field where the planes were parked to see the latest arrivals. We had a lovely gentleman in our Service Department who was always immaculate in his person and dress. When I walked up to the B-24 that he was viewing, this beautiful, naked girl was painted on the airplane. Her naked breasts were like two Seal Beams! He turned to me and said, "Has lovely eyes, hasn't she?"

Tom, after almost 43 years with the company, I could go on and on but will stop with these few memories.

From DOROTHY LOVELADY, Valley Center, CA

Inspecting those PBYs presented some challenges

In World War II, I was working as a Department Clerk in PBY Primary Assembly on the second shift. One evening I heard my Assistant Foreman and the Foreman of Inspection (they were quite buddies) laughing. I asked them what was so funny. They said that one of the women inspectors was inspecting items in the navigation section (she wore "falsies").

PBY-5A Catalina on patrol, 1942-43.
Courtesy Wikipedia

When she pulled herself up from the navigator table to go through the hatch above to inspect other parts, one of her "falsies" slipped down to her waist. Of course, there were fellows in the same area, so they called her "One Hung Low." (There are lots of other things

I remember about Convair, so sometime in my busy days, I'll get a chance to write more.)

From NORM KEITH, Engineering

Nothing like concrete facts

True stories from the "war" years as related to me by several long-time employees with whom I worked with over the years. One female employee who worked the graveyard shift would from time to time get a ride home from her supervisor in his new Cadillac. They arrived home after her husband left for work. A neighbor noticed the 'boss' stayed quite some time so he told the husband who later verified the visits.

One morning he returned home in his work truck, broke the top of the Cadillac's window and filled the car with the product he was supposed to deliver. The car was filled to the top which flattened all four tires from the weight.

Oh, by the way, the husband drove a Redi-mix Concrete truck! Thereafter she was known as "cement ass."

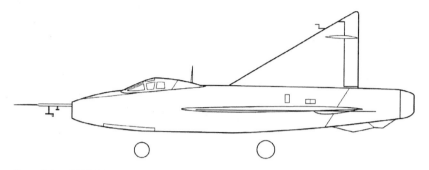

Consolidated XF-92A. This delta-wing interceptor was the precursor to the F-102 Delta Dagger and the F-106 Delta Dart. Courtesy Wikipedia Commons—NASA

From BILL CHANA

From his book *Over the Wing: the Bill Chana Story*, page 58. Used with permission

CHUCKLES WITH FIGHTER LEGENDS

(Preview from page 57. Reference is to the world's first delta wing fighter aircraft. The original concept was developed under a competitive contract at Consolidated Vultee in Downey. Then Convair was given a contract to build a flying mockup of a delta wing aircraft to prove that a delta wing could fly. This was identified as the Convair 7002, then designated as the XF92A.)

In late September, 1949, I was once again assigned to the XF-92 program and was asked to return to Edwards Air Force Base to represent the company during the Air Force flight test program. Captain Chuck Yeager and Lt. Jim Fitzgerald were the two Air Force test pilots assigned to fly the XF-92A's Phase II Test Program. (Yeager had broken the sound barrier in the Bell X-1 in October 1947.) Fitzgerald was flying the prototype T-33 from Wright

19

Field, Dayton, Ohio, to the Lockheed facility at Van Nuys airport; as Jim approached the airport the T-33 went out of control and crashed, killing him instantly. The Air Force immediately assigned Major Frank "Pete" Everest, another seasoned pilot to replace Fitzgerald.

"SOME HUMOR ALWAYS BREAKS THE TENSION"

Yeager and Everest would trade off flying the airplane. When Yeager flew the delta, Everest would fly the chase plane and vice versa. The chase pilot did not sit in on the preflight meetings held in the hangar because it took him some time to ensure that the chase plane was on the operations flight line and ready to go when needed.

One morning at our preflight meeting the Air Force Contracting Officer, Earl Fisher, said, "Captain Yeager, I don't think you should be talking down your data during the flight. This is a secret project and we really don't know who might be listening on your radio frequency." Yeager wanted the Air Force flight test engineer and me to sit in the radio equipped Jeep to write down every word he said so that we could later track it with the photo panel film. Yeager also wanted this done so that he could discuss the flight with his test engineers immediately after landing during the post flight meeting in the hangar. Yeager's response to Mr. Fisher was, "Earl, we will continue doing what we've been doing but I'll add 100 mph to the speed and 10,000 feet to the altitude and that should make any listeners happy."

Yeager released the brakes and started his takeoff roll. Everest was right there in close formation on the wing tip of the Delta. Chuck came over the radio. "Climbing out at 300." Everest immediately said "Chuck I've got 200!" A few seconds later Yeager said "Going through 20,000." Everest was quick to say, "Chuck, I'm going through 10,000." Yeager came back with, "Pete, if you'd get in a little closer, like a fighter pilot should, you'd get the right numbers!" Everest quips back "If I was any closer I'd be in the cockpit with you." At this time they both burst out laughing. True fighter pilots. Two real characters. Yeager and Everest.

CHAPTER 3—1950s

Primary operations at Convair had then became part of General Dynamics (GD), the new Astronautics Division in San Diego, Cape Canaveral, Florida and Vandenberg Air Force Base, California (VAFB) launch vehicle operational bases.

Programs included:

- 340 and 440 Convair-Liner commercial airliners
- Terrier antiaircraft weapon
- T-29 Flying Classroom (modified Convair-Liner)
- POGO vertical takeoff aircraft
- XF-92 experimental aircraft
- F-102 and F-106 delta-wing fighters
- B-36 bomber
- F2Y Sea Dart
- 880 commercial airliner
- Atlas ICBM (Intercontinental Ballistic Missile) weapon
- Atlas space booster

FROM RUTH HAYWARD, PROGRAMMER, RESEARCH ENGINEER IN CONVAIR'S SCIENTIFIC COMPUTING DEPARTMENT, LINDBERGH FIELD

GADGETRY MAYBE A BIT DIFFERENT

In the early fifties, Convair adopted the phrase, "Engineering to the nth degree" to appeal to potential new hires. Recruiters of college engineering students passed out plastic slide rules embellished with the phrase: "When you multiplied two times two, you got 3.7."

In the sixties, Convair's Scientific Computer Department used mainframe IBM computers. Output from computations was stored on 1-inch magnetic tape and printed on an impact printer. This was slow. GD had recently purchased Stromberg-Carlson (SC), who had developed a faster method to print output. It involved projecting a page of data on a CRT and taking a low-grade photo. Faster, but the system, replete with many vacuum tubes, generated much heat. So much heat that often the output paper caught fire, seriously slowing things down. Wasn't long before the impact printers were back in use. One downside was the SC's usefulness of keeping leftover lunch pizza warm for an afternoon snack.

From ED HUJSAK

MIXING WITH THE LEGENDS

Early in my career I had visions of a hundred-mile tower (later reduced to a modest twenty-five miles), the better to launch spacecraft into space from a platform high in the sky. I took a lot of kidding from fellow engineers and put the concept out of thought.

Sir Arthur C. Clark,
Courtesy Wikipedia

Some years later it happened that there was a luncheon meeting at the Smithsonian, the attendees being the museum curator, Phil Culbertson, and Sir Arthur C. Clarke. Sir Arthur said he had an idea for a book and wondered if either of the other two knew of any information regarding very high towers. Phil answered that he knew just the guy and put me in touch with Sir Arthur. I gathered up all the information I had, including an early paper by a Russian who had made the calculations for a cable elevator that extended to geosynchronous orbit. That was exactly what Sir Arthur was looking for. The upshot was the high adventure Sci-Fi book titled "Fountains of Paradise." Sir Arthur's elevator was built of advanced carbon material.

From a personal standpoint for me there ensued a rewarding steady correspondence with Sir Arthur over the years. He lived in Sri Lanka and of course his elevator in the book was anchored in that country.

Today one might argue that with the onset of nano-technology, and specifically nano-engineering, the tower idea may not be that much of a stretch after all. Self-assembly, molecule by molecule, just as cells and sub-cellular construction takes place in life forms, will enable multiple high altitude protuberances from Earth's surface. What they will be used for, however, is anybody's guess.

(On the slight chance you might not be sure who Ed is talking about, Sir Arthur Clark wrote many books, among them *2001: A Space Odyssey.* You may have heard of that.)

FROM DICK RIOS

SKETCH OF AN "OLD PILOT"

Have you ever seen this photo of the "Old Pilot"? During the days at Convair when the F-102s were being delivered to the Air Force, Gene Knowles was in the Flight Test Group [Department Six at Lindbergh Field] and could paint/draw people as well as hardware that appeared, as they were actual photographs. Short story of a long one: Gene would paint a large picture for each F-102 Squadron Ready Rooms when delivery was made and individualize them with their insignias. As I remember the old pilot was modeled from a much younger Eddie J. Carr, an excellent Flight Test Engineer who sat not far from Gene during the conceptual stage of the artwork.

From ED CURRIDEN

SHHH... DON'T SAY THAT WORD...

From *Atlas Recollections—Atlas 50th book 1957-2007*

When I was hired for the Atlas project it was in 1955, I was assigned to the Propulsion Group (very few in the group at that time) and the Atlas was in the mock-up stage. Security was an extremely serious matter and we were lectured time after time that you did not utter the word "Atlas" to anyone...ever. (we could and did call it the Model Seven program within the company).

At that time, I parked my car where Jim's Air is now, as did the majority of us involved in the embryonic stages of the Atlas Project. Well, as circumstances would have it there was a Chevron Station at the entry to Jim's Air. I needed a set of tires to be installed during the work day. There were three brands of tires available at the station and I could only point to the "Atlas" brand and say "I want those." Now, that was the very utmost respect for security in those days. Little did we dream that the word "Atlas" would be known virtually throughout the world during the next 50 years and on.

From DON SULLIVAN

SOME KEY EXPERTISE TO PUT ON YOUR RESUME

My experience on the Atlas program began in 1956 when Atlas A-1 was in the early stages of completion. The engineering department was located in a huge upstairs area above the manufacturing building. I will never forget those days or the following ones when we moved to Edwards Rocket Base with the first Atlas for static firing. Don Waters was our boss with Don Fagan who later took over. I loved every minute that I worked there.

We subsequently were transferred to Vandenberg and prepared ourselves to be able to take the first production missiles to Cheyenne, Wyoming. The "D" series missiles were installed in horizontal launch sites and required special equipment called "The Erection Mechanism." I was given full responsibility to direct the installation, testing and operation of all the equipment required to erect the missile. Once again, I loved every minute spent working on that system. I even prepared a trouble shooting manual called *The Erection Mechanism* by Don Sullivan. I soon became known as "The Erection Expert." That brings me up to the story that I hope you can use and extract the humor that followed.

We worked many hours to activate the first group of Atlases that were being installed in an operational site. Near the completion of our schedule, we were visited by General Curtis LeMay, who was the top general in the Air Force at that time. He arranged for a group of Hollywood entertainers who had just finished putting on a show for the Air Force troops at Warren AFB the previous night. We had specific instructions to have our engineers on station at every support system to explain to the group how everything worked. I was directed to be prepared to erect the missile as soon as the group had completed their tour as a grand finale.

My location was at a panel near the launcher approximately three feet above the main pad floor. When the group reached that location a vision of loveliness stopped right below my position. She placed her delicate little hands on the top of a hard hat that everyone had to wear and in her sweet voice asked me what my job was. I replied "I am the erection expert."

Her response was "Oh, really" with a big smile. General LeMay almost swallowed his cigar, but had to immediately clear the area as I pressed the erection switch and the missile went vertical. The young beauty turned out to be Angie Dickinson.

Now everything I have written brings me to the real punch line that occurred almost 30 years later when an Act of God occurred and I ended up on an aircraft sitting next to Angie. She was unbelievably friendly and talkative. We were sitting in the first row of the aircraft and had no problem being served cocktails. She discussed her recent divorce from the orchestra leader Burt Bacharach while I was dying to mention our previous encounter. Three cocktails later, I mentioned the fact to Angie that we had met before. She looked at me and said she was sorry, but could not remember any previous encounters. I followed up by reminding her of her visit to an Atlas Missile Site with General Curtis LeMay. She immediately responded that she could never forget that event.

I took another gulp of my third cocktail and I asked her if she remembered meeting the "Erection Expert?" She almost choked on her drink and immediately responded "Was that you!!!" She talked about how when the group returned to Hollywood they could not stop talking about the huge missile that they had seen, but she followed those comments by saying **"I met the Erection Expert!"**

FROM KAY QUIJADA

SHOTS COME IN DIFFERENT FORMS

Succumbing to the radio jingle of "Let's All Go to Work for Convair and Make More Money There," I left my secure telephone company job for $1.04 more an hour.

My first day of work in 1956 was in the Engineering Typing Pool for Model Seven in Lindbergh Field's Building Four Mezzanine. I reported to work and found myself alone in a room full of typewriters, desks and chairs. It was the day before the Christmas holiday. I went out to the hall coffee machine to purchase a cup. A few strange young engineers from the vast area I called "the sea of white shirts and drafting tables" had toy water pistols filled with whiskey or similar spirits and were buzzing around the coffee machines asking people if they wanted a "shot." Quickly, I ducked back to my empty office area, blocked the doorway with several wooden chairs, and wondered if I'd made a mistake quitting my other job.

FROM JOHN TRIBE

ONE OF THE STORIES FROM THE EARLY DAYS OF CAPE CANAVERAL ... I WISH WE'D HAD PHOTOS!

In the days before air conditioning, we used to get armadillos in the ready room at Launch Complex-12. They'd get under the lockers, push down with their feet and be impossible to dislodge without tilting the locker. As punishment, we'd often spray paint their shells in our hard hat colors, green (for GD Astronautics) or white with a black stripe for Lockheed, stick the appropriate GDA or Lockheed logo decals on the sides and turn them loose. It was always entertaining to see these live hard hats scurrying off into the boondocks.

From TRUETT SHIPLEY

IS THAT REAL OR FAKE?

Prior to getting a security clearance, my limited information about the Atlas was that it was "very big" which meant to me that one had to stand on a step-ladder to install the nose cone or warhead. Was I ever surprised when in the summer of 1957 I first saw that shiny "tank" in Test Stand-1A at Edwards Rocket Base and realized that the monster shiny tank was really an Atlas. Although my work there that summer demanded that I work on upper levels of TS-1A very near the missile, in lower levels under the test stand and in the TS-1A blockhouse, because I still had no security clearance, nobody was allowed to confirm my suspicions that the shiny tank was really an Atlas. At one point, one smart-ass tongue-in-cheek test engineer, after swearing me to secrecy, revealed that the shiny tank in TS-1A was only a quarter-scale test article.

P.S. You might be interested in knowing that the "smart-ass engineer" was the late John Ona. I sort of figured he was joshing me because that would have meant the full-scale article would be forty feet in diameter. Even so, I'm sure he would have been proud to be cited as that smart-ass test engineer if you want to use his name.

From ED HUJSAK, Predesign and more

Would that Atlas tank hold up???

The Atlas propellant tank concept was the brainchild of Karel Bossart. Realizing that minimizing weight is of paramount importance in the design of rockets, Bossart had the idea that propellant tanks could be built of thin, high-strength stainless steel. They would get their rigidity by employing internal pressure instead of thick walls.

Karel Bossart came rightfully to be known as "The Father of the Atlas." He was a man everyone would like for an uncle; friendly, courteous, a knack for drawing out the best in a person. He often appeared on the design floor to sit down and chat with the engineers, looking to understand how a particular device worked, what its weaknesses were, or how it

Atlas-Agena at Kennedy Space Center with Saturn V Moon Rocket behind. iCrew Photo by Rick Lakin

might fail. Then again, it may have, on occasion, been simply to shore up his own confidence that the designs were in good hands.

Test tanks bore out his theories, and Bossart's ideas were adopted for the Atlas propellant tank design. Needless to say, skepticism about the concept was voiced throughout the industry. Particularly derisive were the German rocket engineers in Huntsville, Alabama, who, being born to the Mercedes mentality, approached missile construction like bridge building.

In a comical incident, General Dynamics had a visitor from the Huntsville structural engineering department. Karel Bossart invited him to examine an Atlas propellant tank that lay horizontal, under pressure, in its cradle outside the manufacturing building. Bossart handed him a sledge hammer and said, **"Go ahead. Hit it."** The engineer bounced the hammer gingerly against the tank, which responded like rubber.

"Harder!" Bossart said.

Again, the visitor swung at the tank, with the same result.

"Hit it hard," Bossart urged, with a grin on his face.

The engineer reared back and swung at the tank with all his strength. The tank remained undamaged. In bouncing back, the hammer left the engineer's hands, tore off his glasses and narrowly missed his head. **"Ja whol!"** he muttered, to accompanying laughter by onlookers.

There are other versions of this story, a result of how folklore tends to change with time, but all are similar.

The incident didn't help relationships with the Huntsville Germans. In the ensuing years, Marshall Space Flight Center dragged its heels in the development of the GD-invented Centaur upper stage, designed along the same principles as Atlas. Frustrated, National Aeronautics and Space Administration (NASA) headquarters transferred the project to its Cleveland center, Lewis Laboratories, where Abe Silverman provided the strong leadership needed for the program.

From Kay Quijada, Personnel. Kearny Mesa-Lindbergh Field

Looking over those possible new hires

Things you don't see anymore. In the early days of Astronautics, employment application forms had a space for an applicant's photo. I remember opening one employment application with a photo of the applicant seated, holding a beer and a leggy lady on his lap. I also recall opening an application from an international applicant whose credits included a yo-yo permit.

I recall working for Engineering Personnel in Lindbergh Field's Building Four and delivering employment applications to Krafft Ehricke, the former German rocket scientist. I would sit in his office, patiently waiting, as he loudly drummed his desk with his large fingers while deep in thought over the applications. I used to wonder if he would burst into song, but no, he never did. I recall his office bookcase filled with books entitled "Mars" and other astronomy subjects.

(From the author: Recent article noting that organizations are not now permitted to ask for a photo with the employment application at the time of interview.)

From Clyde Stroburg

Good design pays off

I worked at General Dynamics (known by many names) for 44 years (counting my two-and-one-half year vacation in the Marine Corps from 1944 to 1946). I started in 1942 as a draftsman in the Engineering Department, and with my schooling in the Marine Corps and extension courses I worked myself up to Senior Design Engineer at my retirement in 1986.

During the early stages of the Atlas Missile Program, our design group did the design of some of the electronic units for Missile Flight Control. One of the men in our group, Dave, was the principal designer of a "package" which became a part of the first Atlas that failed in flight and crashed into the ocean.

A few days later, in a group meeting, our supervisor said, "Dave, you did too good a job on your package. We retrieved it from the crash site, plugged it in, and it worked. It must have been "over-designed." Then everybody laughed. End of story.

From ED HUJSAK

Another of those turtle tales, in your luggage?

Event mid-late fifties from Ed's *A Pig in the Rumble Seat and other short stories*, (2008, a fun read) "San Diego's Missile," p 33.

It happened, at a time when I was supervisor of a propulsion design group, that it became necessary to send a design engineer to Cape Canaveral to oversee the installation of a design change on the Atlas missile. Kenny King was the designer and he was happy to travel, eager to catch the flavor of the program where it really mattered. Kenny was a tall, rangy man, good natured, competent, prematurely gray.

The assigned task completed in the space of two days, Kenny got into his rental car and headed for the Orlando airport. On the way he spied a large turtle by the roadside and immediately decided it would make an admirable souvenir of his trip. He stopped, picked it up and stuffed it into his suitcase, which he ultimately carried to his seat in the aircraft.

Along the way, during flight, the turtle came alive and decided it didn't much like the accommodations. It was a powerful creature as it humped up and finally broke the latches. Kenny spent the rest of the flight holding the suitcase closed with his feet in an ongoing conflict with the turtle.

Kenny and the turtle finally arrived at his home in Rancho Santa Fe. He released it to the fenced back yard. Needless to say, his wife was at a loss regarding how to deal with a suitcase full of clothes laced with turtle excrement, so she threw the whole mess out.

When Kenny later moved to Del Cerro, a settlement in San Diego, he took the turtle with him. Subsequently he moved to Boeing in Washington State, to design airplanes for Boeing, and I have no doubt the turtle now happily resides there.

It was the inspiration for a turtle tale called Phil which you may find under my name on google.

http://ejhujsak.blogspot.com/

From LEROY GROSS

DESIGNING A NEW PAD, MEETING REAL-WORLD CONDITIONS

I started working for Convair at Cape Canaveral on Labor Day, 1957. Of course Labor Day is a holiday so I spent my first day at work with my buddies drinking beer on Cocoa Beach. The next few months I stayed out of sight and learned all about Hangar K. Finally, about Thanksgiving my boss gave me a roll of blueprints and sent me to Launch Complex 11 to help the contractors build the new pad. I had no idea about how to read blueprints (I majored in Physics and Electrical Engineering) but then I found out the electrical contractor didn't know how to read them either. Soon we taught each other what the cryptic symbols meant and proceeded to hook up all the 480 volt circuits and make things work.

The various contractors were from all over the country and had various cultures. One of their customs was to leave the blockhouse (B/H) door open at night when they went home. One morning we came in and found a civet cat (related to a skunk) had entered the B/H overnight. When the first worker came in the next morning the civet cat got excited and headed for the great outdoors, but not before leaving his mark on the floor. Not much work in the B/H that day.

Another morning I arrived to find the contractors had caught a bobcat in a trap and had it in the parking lot. It was very unhappy. After a while somebody took it to the zoo in Titusville.

One day I had to install the control panel for the water system. When I looked at it, it quickly became apparent that it would not work with our plumbing system. I called San Diego and when they checked the part number I was told it was for the water system at Sycamore Canyon. I was also told that they didn't have time to design a new one since they were already working on something else. Tough luck. I would have to design one myself. They really didn't teach me anything like that in college!

After a while we had things more or less working and it was time to erect 3B and launch it. I was put on the Missile Power panel and handed a procedure. I asked "Will we have a practice run?" The answer was "No, just follow the procedure." So I did and when I switched the missile to Internal Power, the battery died. "Redline! Main Missile Battery, Switching to External."

After we detanked and the excitement quieted down, my buddy told me there was an STL (Space Technology Lab, remember that?) guy in the back of the room looking over my shoulder at my meters. A few days later when we tried again I found I could see Mr. STL in the reflection from the glass on one of my meters. I didn't care for people looking over my shoulder so I found that if I leaned a little to the side he couldn't see my meters and second guess what was going on. So much for observers in the back of the room!

From KEITH ANDERSON

Getting ready for Ike

From Atlas Recollections—Atlas 50th book 1957-2007

The flight readiness firing of 3B consisted of a period when all engines were firing and a short period when the sustainer and verniers were firing. The sustainer timer cutoff did not function and the sustainer continued to run much longer than planned. Folk lore has it that Wick Jackson started to sing, "Going to run all day, going to run all night," at which time the test conductor initiated manual shutdown.

The launch of 10B as an orbital vehicle carrying the Eisenhower recording was classified prior to launch. Very few people knew what was going to happen prior to the launch. One of the transplanted German engineers, who didn't know about the mission, was watching the trajectory in real-time and exclaimed, "The rocket ship is going right off the map."

From CLAY PERKINS, Test Labs
Instrumentation Design group

Saving Eisenhower

My first job after getting my MS in physics at the University of Texas was an analysis of the Atlas propellant utilization system (the notorious "PU System" leading to lots of jokes), which led to my crawling inside the engine compartment of the Atlas that launched President Eisenhower's Christmas message to the world in 1958. This was America's answer to Russia's Sputnik.

Atlas missile 10B was sitting on the launch stand with fuel aboard, but the PU system was giving erratic signals. I was rushed to Cape

Canaveral (as it was called then) to help. This was only ten months after I started work. My analysis and tests had focused on helium purge gas dynamics. Things like what happened to the PU output when the tanks were pressurized.

After a day of testing and data analysis, nothing made sense. We weren't told why, but we were being pushed; so, as a last resort I insisted on squeezing into the engine compartment to examine the base of the fuel tank. With fuel aboard, this broke all safety rules, but I eventually got permission.

A safety man had to accompany me; that really helped! Luckily I was pretty skinny; so, with some effort I was able to squeeze up past the sustainer engine by loosening its skirt. With a flashlight, I checked all the purge lines. I found no kinks, dents, or other oddities. I was on a headset, and the whole blockhouse was listening. In desperation, I put my ear against the tank wall, easier said than done, and heard something odd. I pushed talk, "I just listened to the tank. It is going 'bzzzz', instead of 'glug glug glug'."

Long pause, then, "WHAT?"

I repeated and added, "The helium should be coming out in big bubbles, not little ones."

"I think you better come back up here. We need to talk."

By the time I made the long walk back to the blockhouse it was clear to me that the fuel purge tube was partially blocked and that we had to pull the tubing, which meant de-tanking. Seemed simple to me, but all hell broke loose when I walked in and said, "You got to de-tank." The test conductor (don't remember who it was) wasn't having any of that; he knew how critical the schedule was, the rest of us didn't. After a lot of talking, I won (because the TC knew that a working PU was needed to make orbit); so, they started draining the tank, while threatening to fire me if I was wrong!

Hours later a mechanic pulled out the bottom section of tubing and handed it to me. Sure enough, the perfectly standard quarter-inch coupling at the tank wall wasn't! It had a steel plate welded over its end with a tiny hole drilled through it. Just the size to go "bzzzz." The coupling was replaced, fuel tanking started again, I turned from suspected goat to hero, and Eisenhower's voice was launched just in time on December 18, 1958.

Back in San Diego, a witch hunt found that the strange coupling had been made for the Point Loma battleship tank, but no one could explain how it got into the factory parts line.

FROM CURT JOHNSON, CAPE TEST CONDUCTOR

HOW WE GOT IKE'S IMPORTANT MESSAGE TO THE WORLD ON DECEMBER, 18, 1958 LAUNCHED BY ATLAS 10B

Edited from email received in February of 2009, shortly before Curt left us. Only part is "fun" but included more as this was an important milestone.

I was finishing a tour at Holloman Air Force Base, Alamogordo, New Mexico as Test Conductor for Matador missiles developing a guidance system. I had a choice of going back to the snow of Akron, Ohio or going to San Diego for a secret missile development program as an Research and Development (R&D) Senior Engineer. I chose the warmth of San Diego.

I was placed into a field service group and told that I was a candidate for a Test Conductor at the Atlantic Missile Range in Florida but I could not be sent there for one year since they had relocated me to San Diego. There was very little to do in San Diego for field troops and there were no overall schematics of the Missile and Ground system so Walt Hicks, Jim Brown and I started making schematics. In the process, we found many errors in the design between the missile and the ground control equipment. These schematics were invaluable when we started checking out the ground system.

At the Cape, the crew of each launch site reflected the attitude of the supervision on that site. One site would have an almost formal dinner to celebrate a launch. Another site would have a beach party immediately following the launch while still another site would have no dinner or party at all. My site had the beach parties with cases of beer and sandlot softball games. Some of the crew got into trouble at home because of these parties so the solution was to have the families of the crew watch the launch from the beach where the party was going to be held. Those parties were outstanding.

In October 1958, we performed a tanking and a static firing on each missile before launch. I had missile 6B on the launch pad of Launch Complex-12. During the static firing, we had a fire on the sustainer engine. If we pulled the missile from the pad and took it back to a hangar it would take a week to get back to the pad and then re-do all the tests which would interfere with the next launch of 10B. Trav Maloy, the Chief Test Conductor (my boss) told me that we could not slide the launch of 10B. He asked if we could change out the sustainer engine on the pad. I said we would look into it.

George Page, my propulsion engineer, Carl Striby the launcher engineer, the shop supervisor and I got together and kicked around a way to do this as the missile would have to be partially staged. We decided we could and Trav blessed it. The launcher hold-down heads were held in place prior to launch with static links. We disconnected these links from the heads. The staging fittings (booster to sustainer) were all opened. A support structure was placed under the sustainer engine. The missile stabilization cylinders were slowly pressurized which lifted the tank and sustainer. The static links were re-installed at this extended position.

The tallest, skinniest mechanic was threaded up between the sustainer engine and the booster so he could disconnect the plugs and propellant lines from the sustainer. This was done and a block and tackle was attached to the top of the sustainer. The support structure was removed from beneath the sustainer engine. Padded poles were placed on each side of the sustainer engine down into the flame bucket. The sustainer engine was slowly lowered down through the flame bucket using the block and tackle. One day later a new sustainer engine was snaked up into the booster section and the process reversed. The following day the leak check was completed on the new sustainer and the fourth day we ran x-minus one day for a static firing.

The third day after that we launched 6B and the bird flew like a charm. The replacement of 6B's sustainer engine on the launch pad was a far greater crew performance than the launch of 10B. Having done what we did on 6B equipped the crew to perform without question in the preparation of 10B for launch.

I was never told that 10B was going into orbit but I and most of the engineers in the launch crew drew that conclusion from the events of processing the missile. The launch date was held to be holy. I had authority to do almost anything to the missile or the launch pad. The directions from my leader were beyond, in some cases, some safety margins, i.e., flying without "in flight" destruct capability from the ground. The fact that there was a tape recorder aboard the missile would make no sense if 6000 miles downrange was the end of the trip.

The launch crew engineers followed my direction without question, doing things such as clipping wires, simulating data used to determine the missile was ready to launch and pretending that equipment was on the missile when it was not. Even the inspection department followed my instructions and assisted in covering up hoaxes regarding the configuration of the missile.

The Air Force officer (he knew the missile's goal and the changes being made) in charge of the Test Wing at the Atlantic Missile Range was astounded that I and the launch crew could violate so many "no-no's" and his high paid monitors did not catch us.

More about Atlas 10B launch

The new, longer nosecone would not clear the guard rails on the eleventh deck. The crane hook was lassoed and wrapped. The bottom of the nosecone was held out and then up by four technicians as the crane was processed in. The new payload was never seen by the crew before it was opened that day. The technicians went throughout the missile and clipped off any unused brackets with tin snips; no real records.

Bob Shoff (autopilot engineer) determined the wire number for the sustainer cutoff signal from the guidance system to the engine relay box, found the wire, clipped it, insulated the two ends and poked them back into the wire bundle. Jim Starkey (complex electrical engineer) simulated the sustainer cutoff signal manually, was under the blockhouse floor, and below my chair and activated the signal on my cue, during the autopilot loop test.

The loop test was given a "go" by the evaluators. The range safety receiver was removed from the missile after launch and x-minus-1 day tests were done. The receiver was stowed and locked in the inspection file cabinet at the pad by Stretch Talbert, the Inspection supervisor.

Four days before launch, an radio frequency (RF) engineering supervisor from San Diego and two military people showed up to install a package on the missile. They were back on launch x-minus-1 day second shift; after being on the missile they came back to my desk in the ready room.

The one military guy said "I almost screwed up the whole launch, I hit the erase button accidentally but the phase I deleted was not important." That nailed down the fact that it was a voice recorder and the bird had to be going into orbit.

During the countdown, I told Jim Harrington III (crew Range Safety engineer) that the range safety package had been removed and that the range was not going to see any signal. He should remain calm and report to me that they had given him a "no go." This he did. I waited about a minute and then called the Air Force SRO (Superintendent Range Operation) and told him that I had received a "no" signal report from the range safety folks but I was requesting permission to launch in hopes of the signal coming up after launch.

There was a lot of gasping in the blockhouse of such an unheard-of request. In about another minute the SRO called me back and said I was approved to launch without the range safety "go." That got an even louder gasp from folks in the blockhouse.

After the launch the three guys who had installed the package came and got me and took me to their trailer which was on a net to Perth, Australia, which was to be the first to dump President Eisenhower's message. Shortly after we got there, the message came through that

Perth had dumped the message and here it was. That was the convincing item that said 10B was a success.

Dwight D. Eisenhower, President of the United States from 1953-1961

Message from the 34ᵗʰ President of the United States conveyed from space: "This is the President of the United States speaking. Through the marvels of scientific advance, my voice is coming to you via a satellite circling in outer space. My message is a simple one: Through this unique means I convey to you and all mankind, America's wish for peace on Earth and goodwill toward men everywhere."

I received messages from all over the country from people I had worked with and newspaper articles from my home town in Ohio and other papers around the country. The next day we had to clean up the pad and get ready for the next launch but we all felt good about being in the forefront of the missile business. Those Atlas early years were the greatest in my life, I feel very lucky to have been there.

From MERCURY ASTRONAUTS FIRST ONE + ALAN SHEPARD

From ATLAS MERCURY PROGRAM

REMEMBER THE 1ST ASTRONAUT? A CHAP NAMED JOSÉ JIMÉNEZ?

Bill Dana (left) as José Jiménez on The Danny Thomas Show. Courtesy Wikipedia

Many were part of the Atlas programs which would send the Mercury Astronauts into orbit. This program was high publicity, especially as the Soviets had already placed their man into earth orbit. A memorable part of press activities then was when we would hear directly from the First Astronaut, a chap who introduced himself with the line "My nayne Jose' Jimenez." He was a character created by Bill Dana, a regular comedian on the Steve Allen evening show.

To hear directly from Jose (interviewed by Ed Sullivan), check

https://youtube.com/watch?v=i6ckW7uRRNw

From *We Seven by the Astronauts Themselves*, Simon & Schuster 1962, From chapter by Alan Shepard, Jr. P 240, "The First American." Shepard was the first Mercury Astronaut to fly into space in a suborbital mission atop the Redstone rocket. Virgil "Gus" Grissom flew a second suborbital mission before all succeeding Mercury flights began atop the Atlas.

OR MAYBE SHEPARD WAS NOT THE 1ST U.S ASTRONAUT (CORRECTO JOSE?).

Along about this time Shepard and Grissom went through a little routine to relax everyone in the van, I had been much amused by an 'Astronaut' recording which featured a Spanish Astronaut named

José Jimenez. When someone asked José in an interview what he was going to going to do on his epic flight, he answered in a poignant Spanish accent, "I'm going to cry a lot." (I saved that line and used it on Gus when he went up—see the following chapter.)

At one point in the brief routine, Shepherd—still imitating the Jimenez record—started to tick off in his own best Spanish accent the qualities a good Astronaut must have. He listed the obvious ones, like courage, perfect vision and low blood pressure. Then he added, "And you've got to have four legs."

"Why four legs," asked Gus, who was playing the straight man.

"They really wanted to send a dog," Al answered, "but they thought that would be too cruel.'"

MORE ABOUT THE ASTRONAUTS

MORAL RESPONSIBILITY, A SAN DIEGO REVELATION

From *The Astronaut Wives Club* by Lily Koppel, p 39, chapter "The Cookies"

"Soon the astronauts were off to the Convair plant in California. Here was where they were building the Atlas rocket that would fulfill Project Mercury's goal of putting a man into orbit around the Earth before the Russians did. As usual at these Astro-junkets, the red carpet was rolled out and the boys were put up in the first-class Kona Kai Resort, a tropical oasis of lush gardens with torchlights and white-sand beaches on the shores of the Pacific at the tip of Shelter Island off San Diego.

Alan Shepard got a room with twin beds, which didn't exactly fit his plans for the evening, so he asked to switch rooms with Scott Carpenter, who'd been assigned a full-sized bed. Scott handed over his key and Alan headed off to his new room. Why did Alan need the extra mattress space? As the story went, Alan had gone across the border and picked up a *chiquita* in a bar in Tijuana, the den of sin for many a lonely sailor stationed in San Diego.

In the middle of the night, John Glenn was woken up by a phone call from John "Shorty" Powers, the NASA press officer known as the 'voice of the astronauts and Mercury Control,' who had been a cheerleader in high school. Shorty had gotten a call from a paper that was ready to run a story, complete with incriminating photos.

John was livid. He convinced the reporter and the photographer and the editor, who he got out of bed, not to run the story. It was a matter of national security. The next morning, John asked for a 'séance,' which was what the seven astronauts called their closed-door meetings. This one would be forever known as the Kona Kai Seance. As John saw it, any astronaut who couldn't keep his 'pants zipped' threatened to ruin everything and squash America's opportunity to beat the Russians, not only in space but also on the grounds of moral superiority. They all had a responsibility to the country to be the wholesome heroes they were sold as. John went head-to- head with Alan over the issue.

They didn't come to any agreement, but the overriding feeling was that any extracurricular monkey business was each man's own private affair, so long as he kept it out of sight."

From BOB MOBERLY

1957—Point Loma tanking tests, Test Engineer working in Department 756.

1959—Vandenberg AFB, Design Engineer in Department 537 working for Don Jenkins.

EARLY FUN, SORT OF, WITH THE ATLAS

I started out in the Systems Test Lab in 1956. My first task was to design and build a stretch system for the first Atlas tank to be filled with liquid oxygen. We developed the tanking procedure and equipment in our tests at Point Loma that supported the first Atlas launch (4A). We learned how to do this without clean rooms!

In 1959, when the Air Force destroyed an Atlas on 65-2 at Vandenberg AFB, during a filming of a Perry Mason show, I was the only civilian called into evaluate the damage. Some fella by the name of Jim Dempsey called me and told me not to give them an estimate of the damage.

FROM DAN HEALD, ATLAS PROPULSION GROUP

IT PAYS TO HAVE A GOOD EXCUSE,

His story from the Atlas Recollections—Atlas 50th book 1957-2007

To prepare for the first Atlas launch, of 4A, in 1957, I went to the Cape to check out the tanking units. They found other GSE to check so they would not let me go home for three weeks. But Sam Merkowitz, the launcher inventor, went home after one weekend! Why?

Sam told me, "I was brewing beer in the bath tub. Either they let me go bottle it or repaint the inside of my house."

CHUCK DEMUND

Here are his GD recollections from his book *My Accidental Life.* Used with his permission.

On December 16, 1957—five days before my 25th birthday—the Atlas, America's first intercontinental ballistic missile, flew successfully for the first time at Cape Canaveral in Florida. That same day, I interviewed with the new Convair Astronautics Motion Picture Department at Eagles Hall, 733 Eighth Avenue in San Diego,

California. (No way I wouldn't get hired on such a celebratory day!!) Head of the department was Eugene Keefer, possibly the most entrepreneurial person ever to work in aerospace. He was at the Cape for the launch and his assistant hired me. I met Gene upon his return and my life would never be the same.

My first assignment was as an archivist, responsible for logging, cataloging and security for all movie film generated on the Atlas program. My pay was to be $2.35 an hour. As a part of the overall Atlas contract the company was required by the Air Force to make quarterly film reports on program progress...or lack thereof! The first two attempts to fly had ended in very spectacular explosions well within view of the press and half of the citizens of central Florida.

Only a few weeks after I joined the department—which at the time numbered about fifteen or twenty cinematographers, writers, editors, and the like—one of our supervisors had a heart attack while on travel at Cape Canaveral. He was to remain in hospital there for a number of weeks and stood to miss the graduation ceremonies for two of his children.

Keefer called me in and ordered me to film both ceremonies, with sound, get the film processed ASAP at a local lab, jump on the Air Force shuttle flight to the Cape with a 16mm projector and show their father the films in his hospital room.

That's where I met Hal Reavely, a retired Navy Chief Petty Officer, who also would have a great influence on my early career and become a valued friend. I'm sure seeing the film of his kids' graduations helped his recovery. I'm not sure whether the job was charged to the Air Force or not!

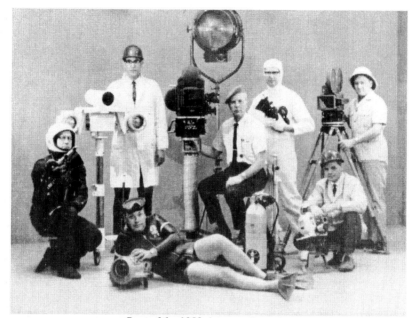

Part of the 1958 Astronautics crew.
Hal Reavely is wearing the beret; I'm the diver on the floor.

The Atlas ICBM program had the highest national defense priority in the late 1950s, so just about anything went, as long as we could claim to be "documenting" the effort. Adding to the fun was the Secret classification of the project. (For a while it was a security violation to even mention the program name, Atlas.)

Each flight test generated thousands of feet of 16mm and 35mm film. All the test film had to be escorted from Cape Canaveral to the labs in Hollywood. There it was segregated from all of their other work, processed and duplicated, and then hand-carried back to San Diego or to other Air Force locations for review. Every roll and foot and frame of film had to be accounted for, even blank ones! I had plenty to do! In four years of being responsible for this accounting we never lost a frame.

Much later I heard harrowing stories of our large, locked red metal film shipping boxes being accidentally left in rental cars, and even on the tarmac at the Mexico City airport when a courier couldn't convince the airline folks that it had to be on the plane with him.

All these stories had happy endings, though, and the Atlas program thrived. Chuck's book is available at amazon.com.

From TOM LEECH, a more current Chuck DeMund story

You never know who you'll meet at California campgrounds

A few years ago, my wife and I with a couple of pooches stopped in at the Dana Point State Campground. That's a popular camping venue as it's right at the ocean, so popular we couldn't get a campsite right at the shoreline. It's a nifty campground no matter where you plop your RV. We strolled around, taking in the views and passed by one large RV at the shore with an empty space next to it. No surprise and the reservation would clearly be filled in later afternoon.

We chatted a bit with the friendly woman in the RV. She alerted us that that empty camp site was reserved for another RV, owned by a friend. However it appeared the friend was not able to get there that night, and if we wanted to camp there we could do it. Yippee!

We moved our RV right next to hers and shared her campfire. During our evening chat, I mentioned that I had spent many years with GD in San Diego. "Interesting," she said, "So did my husband." Hmmm… and what is his name. "Chuck DeMund, maybe you knew him. He'll be arriving later to join us for our evening camp out."

Talk about a coincidence! I knew Chuck well from his career in the photo lab at Kearny Mesa Building Four (and other locales). He joined us and we shared lots of GD stories that evening. (I doubt I made any pages in his book though.)

ED "SPIKE" WOLFENSBERGER

SUPERVISORS AT WORK

At GD/Astronautics "up on the hill" as it was known in 1958, I was a member of the Landlines Instrumentation group for Atlas where there seemed to always be some interesting or unusual thing happening as we tried to accurately measure temperatures, pressures, strain, flow, position, volume and sound. Those instrumentation engineers worked well together helping each other like a well-oiled machine under the guidance of Don Wilson and John Hughes.

The main supervisor was D.G. Wilson who along with his assistant John Hughes was as great a set of bosses that you could have. They were never hesitant to dig in and help you get the job done.

D.G. (Darn Good) Wilson) was a tremendous help any time you ran into difficulties getting your job done. He would drop by your desk nearly every day to ask how things were going and if you were having any difficulties. He carried a pad of yellow paper upon which he wrote down in large crawly, every-other-line handwriting listing any of your difficulties. It might be, for instance, getting a new transducer hurriedly processed through its calibration process.

He would usually return to his desk with that information where you would find him talking on the telephone with his feet upon his desk finding who to see and what to do to solve your problem. Shortly afterwards he would appear back at your desk with another sheet of yellow paper giving the steps to follow to break the system log-jam that was holding you up.

One morning as we came to work a couple of the guys came in a little late and were caught by a newly implemented gate-check at the back gate! When they came into the group, growling about it, one of the other engineers there stood up and announced "Gate Check Time" and everybody got up and walked out the side door and over to go out the nearest side gate and then on around the plant to the front reentering at the lobby entrance where we all had to sign in.

We went back to our work and about 10:00 am, D.G. Wilson and his assistant John Hughes called us all into a conference room to ask what the heck was going on. Don said he was there early and knew darned well that most of us were already there. And then he figured it out! "OK!" Shaking his head. "Back to work! I'll take care of this."

FROM TOM PHILLIPP

BIG BLAST, EARLY

I had the dubious distinction of having been on the launch team in the blockhouse for what I think has been to this day the biggest explosion at ground level in the history of the Cape (September, 1959), Atlas-Able 9C for Project Ranger, the first lunar impact payload program. The concussion was great enough to suck air out of the blockhouse closed doors, and when the equalizing repercussion sprung the doors open, it sent the security guard in front of them spread-eagle on the floor. We later kidded him about being the first man propelled by an Atlas, not John Glenn.

FROM TED LAMOUREUX Test Labs

GET THOSE GADGETS CLAIMED EARLY

Like many people in the Test Labs I have more than a few stories of things that went wrong during my testing of various missile components and subsystems. I guess the one thing that stands out the most is what someone else did to me.

In 1959, I was still on nights in the Test Labs and was responsible for testing missile batteries. In fact I did a test on the main missile battery (my report was published and is available through the Ft. Belvoir Defense Technical Information Center Library) and as a result I was assigned to perform a special combined environmental test on another main missile battery.

This test was to be performed simultaneously at temperature, altitude and vibration. We checked around with the other engineers in the labs and found that no one had previously done this type of test. So I designed and had built a special fixture to be used on the C-25 vibration exciter. It consisted of a circle of aluminum on top of a flat plate and had pipe welded into the circle for a hose to a vacuum pump. On top of the circle we could place a fiberglass dome previously used for antenna testing. Then a portable temperature chamber was placed over the fixture. Evaluation testing of the design found that there were no resonant frequencies inherent in the design within our test range. The test went off without a hitch.

Now forward a number of years to about 1985. I picked up a copy of The Convair News and lo and behold there is a picture of the test fixture that I had designed, had built and used. A young engineer (who shall remain nameless) had applied for and received a patent for my design. At least I had the satisfaction of knowing that the design was more than acceptable.

Here is the famous spiral staircase, in Building Two at Astronautics Kearny Mesa.

FROM PAUL HORIO, KEARNY MESA STRUCTURAL DESIGN

MILLION TO ONE COINCIDENCE.

In the summer of 1958, I had just graduated from University of Dayton (Ohio) and I was at my first job at Wright Patterson AFB. I met Tom Leech who was there for a summer job between his Junior and Senior years at Purdue University. When he left to go back to Purdue I never imagined in a million years that I'd see him again.

The next year I got a job offer from General Dynamics Astronautics, so I drove to San Diego, walked into their new employees reporting room and who do I see but Tom Leech, also signing in. Now that's a "Million-to-One Coincidence." (I worked at GD/Astronautics from 1959 thru 1967.)

AND A RELATED TALE...

SEARCH FOR LOVE IN CATALINA, ISLAND OF ROMANCE...NOT!

The song goes: "Twenty-six miles across the sea, Santa Catalina is a-waitin' for me, Santa Catalina, the island of romance, romance, romance, romance..."

In June of 1959, I became house-mates with Tom Leech, Dick Ladson, and Gary Wetmore, all of us new-hires at Astronautics. We first rented an apartment in North Park, then in September, we moved to a house right on the boardwalk in North Mission Beach. Labor Day week-end arrived and here we were...four aerospace engineers from the Mid-West or East on our first venture together on a boat trip to Catalina with a guarantee (based on the song) of tropical island romance.

To our utmost disappointment, we ended up, not in the bedrooms of some nubile lasses, but on a hard concrete outdoor patio for which we had to pay to stay. Oh, well, that's life. But our Bota bags were always full of wine, and the California girls, sunny beaches and the warm ocean couldn't be beat.

AEROSPACE ENGINEERS GET LOST IN CLAIREMONT ON WAY HOME.

In 1959, Tom Leech, Dick Ladson, Gary Wetmore, another engineer named Bill, and I would car-pool from Mission Beach to Astronautics at Kearny Mesa. Many of you may recall that on Friday afternoons, various vendors, suppliers, and subcontractors would host "hospitality suites" at the hotel on Clairemont Mesa Blvd. across the 805 Freeway.

Since we were "very dedicated engineers," determined to be up to date on the latest and newest data and products, we would devote ample amount of time at various "hospitality suites" absorbing knowledge accompanied by complementary spirits. Perhaps more spirits than knowledge.

On one occasion, after enjoying such an event, we five learned aerospace engineers, some with advanced degrees from MIT or Rensselaer Poly Tech, managed to get completely lost going home among the residential streets of the Clairemont community.

Note: We blame the fact that we didn't have a GPS.

From TOM LEECH, Test Lab, Kearny Mesa

Beach party with the Astronauts?

In the fall of 1959, as Paul Horio noted, four of us GD new engineers rented a house on Oceanfront Walk in North Mission Beach. On weekends two of the guys, Dick and Gary, often spent some fun time with the Convair Water Ski Club. They skied on Mission Bay, landing and returning from the beach next to the Bahia Hotel.

One Saturday, after an afternoon of skiing, they came back to our rental with an amazing tale. Joining the usual GD skiers was a troupe of visitors, the Mercury Astronauts, Alan Shepard, John Glenn and crew. They had come to San Diego to check out the Astronautics Division's facilities, the Atlas vehicles which would launch them into space, and to meet with key Astro people.

Someone had invited them to go water skiing with the GD club, so there they were. After a full afternoon of skiing, chatting, and general loafing, our two roomies Dick and Gary told them about our digs just a few blocks away and suggested they pop on over for an evening beach party. They thought that was a great idea and a fun break from a busy week. Except, their trip head reminded them that they had another mandatory social visit that same evening. So the beach party didn't happen, leaving me with a major-league DARN! as I had missed the chance to spend an evening having fun with those about-to-be-super-famous astronauts.

Gus's speech stirs up the troops

From my article "When Aerospace Was King" San Diego Magazine, December 1997

In the fall of 1959 the seven Mercury astronauts came to Kearny Mesa. They would be riding into space aboard our Atlas missiles. All seven were trooped out for us workers to see and cheer. This particular event was documented by Tom Wolfe in *The Right Stuff*, as was the whole Mercury program, peccadillos and all. While some of the astronauts, particularly Alan Shepard and John Glenn, were always eager to give speeches, Gus Grissom didn't like that part at all.

According to Wolfe: "...like handing him a knife and asking him to cut a main vein." But he was obligated to say something. He was introduced, stepped forward, looked out over the crowd of several thousand employees, gulped and said, "Well...Do good work!" The whole speech.

Wolfe noted the workers' reaction to Grissom's stirring comment: "They started cheering as if they'd just heard the most moving and inspiring message of their lives: Do Good Work! After all, it's Little Gus's ass on top of our rocket!" That phrase became the slogan for the Atlas team, with huge banners appearing in assembly areas, tags on parts, and documents all flagging out "Do Good Work." Gus' words were right up there with "Damn the Torpedoes—full speed ahead!" as far as we were concerned.

FROM DICK LADSON, ENGINEERING KEARNY MESA

GETTING ACQUAINTED WITH THE ASTRONAUTS, ON THE WATER

(EDITOR—THE REAL VERSION OF WHAT HAPPENED WITH THOSE MERCURY CHAPS)

Back in 1959 I was a young engineer working at Convair Astronautics in San Diego. My job was to analyze telemetry data from test launches of the Atlas missile, which was the vehicle designed to lift the original astronauts into space.

It was an exciting time as a young bachelor living in the great city of San Diego in a beachfront cottage in Mission Beach. Convair had a great policy of investing all proceeds from its vending machines into an extensive recreation program, which included a water ski club. The company provided two wonder-

John Glenn in foreground. Dick Ladson on left. Photo courtesy Dick Ladson.

ful Chris-Craft inboard ski boats and all gas and maintenance needed to operate them. This was a first class operation that I exploited to the fullest, skiing every weekend on Mission Bay. As a result I became an accomplished skier.

One week the seven original Mercury astronauts visited the Convair plant in Kearny Mesa on a public relations tour prior to a pending test launch of the Atlas. They spoke to us workers, and I will never forget their statement to us, which was simple and profound: "**Do good work**". How appropriate for someone whose lives depended on the workmanship of others That statement epitomized a popular "ism" of the time, "KISS, Keep It Simple, Stupid".

Later, the astronauts expressed a desire to try water skiing, so they participated in one of the outings of our ski club, and I had the privilege of serving as their boat driver. Being athletic in body and competitive in spirit they would settle for nothing less than skiing on one ski. I remember vividly watching John Glenn and Alan Shepard skimming along the water, each trying to outperform the other.

In an effort to be hospitable, I invited the astronauts to my abode for cocktails and dinner. They expressed eagerness to join us at the beach, but their advisor said not possible due to another Astronaut commitment.

FUN ON THE JOB

From DICK LADSON

Frisky times for new engineers

As a hot new engineer at Convair in 1959, while still an innocent, I was still looking for the love of my life. One night at a Friday night dance in Kearny Mesa I thought I had found her. At first she rejected my advances, refusing to dance with me, but at the end of the dance she approached me and asked for a ride home. I recognized a come-on when I saw one so I agreed, even though she lived <u>45 miles</u> in the wrong direction.

While driving I pondered how to get her to ask me in for milk and cookies, when she announced, "You know Richard, I have mono-nucleosis and hepatitis, which are highly contagious." I was blown away; she actually did care for me and was truly interested in my health. She could have just ravished me for my body, but she exercised restraint for my benefit.

I responded, "Well, could I have your phone number?"

She said "Of course, but mono sometimes lasts up to six months, so why don't you call me then." Then she gave me her number; I will never forget it, WE-6-1212. Unfortunately our romance withered because every time I called her, all she wanted to do to do was talk about the weather.

Dick Ladson, the swinging engineer

From CHUCK DEMUND, Video Photographer

John Glenn's Recovery... and Mission Bay Recall?

From *My Accidental Life,* by Chuck DeMund. Get on Amazon.com

It was my good fortune to draw the recovery ship assignment, along with Hal Reavely and Blake Barton, both retired Navy photographers. We boarded the *USS Randolph*, a World War II vintage *Essex* class carrier, in Norfolk, Virginia and headed to the Caribbean. There were many delays in Glenn's launch, some lasting up to a week. With us aboard the carrier were pool film cameramen from the TV networks and from the newsreels—remember them? On launch day they were confined to a raised platform on the flight deck. Because we were the official NASA film crew, I had the run of the deck.

When John finally flew, his Mercury capsule landed many miles from us and a Navy destroyer picked him up. He was ferried to the *USS Randolph* by helicopter. Arriflex motion picture camera on my shoulder, I ran to the door of the helicopter as soon as it touched down. The newsreel film shows me

Frame from film "Friendship 7" – from my Arriflex - Courtesy NASA

filming John as he exited the aircraft and walked to a small podium to pose, sign some documents and shake hands with the NASA and Navy dignitaries on hand.

About an hour later I was allowed into the ship's sickbay to shoot more film. As I entered, John looked up and asked, "How's the water skiing on Mission Bay, Chuck?" I was pretty amazed that he remembered me and that I had been with him when he and the other six Mercury astronauts had spent a week in San Diego almost a year earlier. Our film was flown to the mainland by Navy jet. When I returned to San Diego a couple days later and went to a theater I saw my own footage of that sickbay incident as a part of the newsreel piece about John's flight.

A writing and editing crew worked night and day in San Diego to complete our hour-long "Friendship 7" film for NASA. When it was done it ran on all three U. S. TV networks, in prime time, on the same night. I know of no other documentary film that has ever been given that kind of exposure.

From PAUL HORIO, Astronautics Structural Design Group

The Golden Days of Aerospace...Days of Yore

I was hired by GD/Astronautics in 1959 after one year engineering experience at Wright Patterson AFB. Namely, I was totally green behind my ears in engineering. Unbelievably, about three or four months into my job in the Structural Design Group, I was sent to attend a three day Cryogenic Engineering Conference in beautiful Boulder, Colorado. And all I had to do was listen to the presentations and absorb information.

Even more amazing is that they put me in First-Class on a Red Carpet flight (they actually rolled out a red carpet from the terminal to the aircraft), and I stayed at a very fancy, expensive-looking hotel. I don't know what the per-diem was, but I certainly didn't starve during the trip. (I swear, I'm not related to Jim Dempsey).

Those were golden days of yore for Aerospace. Can you imagine this happening today?

CHAPTER 4—1960s

Primary operations at General Dynamics (GD) Convair and Astronautics Divisions, multiple Atlas weapon bases, Cape Canaveral and Vandenberg (VAFB).

Programs included:

- Atlas ICBM (Intercontinental Ballistic Missile) weapon
- Atlas space booster
- Centaur upper stage rocket
- 880 and 990 commercial airliners

Astronautics Executive staff at the new San Diego Kearny Mesa facility, likely about '59-60. (from left) Ernie Hill, Frank Traversi, Grant Hansen, Sam Ackerman, Phil Harr, Charlie Ames, Bill Van Horn, Cushman Dow, Bill Patterson, Mort Rosenbaum, Elwood Bryant and Jim Dempsey (Astro top exec). Photo Courtesy General Dynamics

From BOB EIDSON

CENTAUR TRANSLATED INTO ENGLISH

I have many memories of the early days of Atlas and Centaur having signed on with Convair on February 14, 1958 fresh out of the Army Corps of Engineers as a First Lieutenant. I was hired by Don Jenkins and went to work as an engineer in the Atlas Propulsion group at the Lindbergh Field facility. After the move to the new Kearny Mesa facility, we became Convair Astronautics Division.

Centaur Rocket Installation in PSL - Propulsion Systems Laboratory #1. The RL-10 Rocket was developed by Pratt and Whitney in the late 1950s and tested at the Lewis Research Center (now known as the John H. Glenn Research Lewis Field). Courtesy NASA

When the Centaur Research and Development program began in 1960 under the Defense Advanced Research Projects Agency (DARPA), I was assigned to the Centaur Propulsion Group and spent many months developing designs for liquid oxygen (LO$_2$) and liquid hydrogen (LH$_2$) propellant feed systems. This included Propellant Tank mounted, turbine driven Boost Pumps which supplied the Pratt and Whitney (P&W) RL-10 Rocket Engine with propellants meeting the Pump Inlet requirements for the two engines.

We had Test Stands at Point Loma for feed systems tests and then transitioned to new Test Stands at Edwards Rocket Site and a vertical test stand at the P&W facility in West Palm Beach, Florida. I spent a lot of time at all of these facilities and witnessed both failures and successes while proofing the feed systems designs.

The P&W vertical stand experienced two successive explosive failures due to failure of the RL-10 engines to reliably ignite. The third and subsequent firings were successful after the igniter was redesigned. Then a heavyweight vehicle insulated with several inches of spray-on foam was activated at Sycamore Canyon along with the necessary Steam Ejectors to simulate a Space Environment for the RL-10 Engines. That test program was very successful though a few problems were encountered along the way.

During one of the early tests, an LH_2 leak occurred at the outlet of the LH_2 Boost Pump due to a defective seal. The hot Boost Pump Turbine exhaust ignited the LH_2 and resulted in activation of the test stand Firex system which dumped large quantities of Water onto the Test Vehicle. The fire was quickly extinguished. About an hour after the test was aborted, Krafft Ehricke, then the Centaur Program Manager, showed up. I escorted Ehricke, one of the German Rocket Scientists who came to the US along with Werner Von Braun, to the Water Soaked Test Vehicle. He was quite agitated and spoke to me in German "Vas ist los" which I think was "What Is Going on?" in English.

I responded with an explanation of what had happened and he quickly calmed down when he realized that the damage was minimal, mostly some burning of the Foam Insulation. There were numerous sensors to detect leaking H_2 but they caused such frequent false alarms, due to their sensitivity, that the Test Conductor had disabled them to enable the Test Program to proceed without interruption. Those sensors were redesigned and reactivated for further Test Operations.

I recall driving to Sycamore for a pre-test meeting when I heard on my Car Radio the Speech which President J F Kennedy made announcing that the US was going to land Men on the Moon before 1970.

On September 12, 1962, President John F. Kennedy delivered this speech before a crowd of 35,000 people in the Rice football stadium. Courtesy NASA

"We choose to go to the Moon! We choose to go to the Moon in this decade and do the other things, not because they are easy, but because they are hard; because that goal will serve to organize and measure the best of our energies and skills, because that challenge is one that we are willing to accept, one we are unwilling to postpone, and one we intend to win."

FROM DICK MARTIN

BEING THE STUCKEE PRESENTER

From Atlas Recollections—Atlas 50th book 1957-2007

About 1960 GD got an urgent call to come back to Strategic Air Command (SAC) headquarters to explain why the Atlas would not blow over in ground winds. I was the stuckee and went with an Air Force major from Ballistic Missile Defense (BMD). As we were settled in the conference area five floors below ground and watched a wall map of the world full of lights, the deputy SAC commander opened his adjoining door and for five minutes berated a Department of Defense (DOD) undersecretary. He then stomped down to the front of the room and said **"I hope you don't have a bunch of #$%&#$ to tell me!"**

The major, who was supposed to give a ten minute introduction, got up and said "I have Mr. Martin from General Dynamics" and sat down. I was sure glad I had spent the weekend rehearsing my presentation, and after shaking for a couple of minutes, delivered a convincing story as to why they didn't need to worry about Atlas blowing over.

FROM BOB WARD

From *The Light Stuff: Space Humor—from Sputnik to Shuttle*, by Bob Ward

STRAIGHT TALK (PAGE 122)

At a Project Mercury press conference, a reporter asked what might result if the retro rockets used to slow the spacecraft refused to fire. Was there any method of rescue?

Replied James Dempsey of General Dynamics Astronautics: "I would send for a priest."

TAKING NO CHANCES (PAGE 126).

Astronaut Leroy Gordon "Gordo" Cooper, Jr. had visited an aerospace plant in San Diego (e.g., GD Astro) for the ceremonial rollout of the Atlas rocket that was to loft his Mercury capsule into orbit. Taking a felt-tip pen, he drew an arrow on the side of the rocket pointing to its nose and wrote this instruction:

"Launch *this* way—G. Cooper, pilot"

FROM MERCURY ASTRONAUT WALLY SCHIRRA

ABOUT SITTING ON TOP OF THAT ATLAS RIGHT BEFORE BLAST-OFF

From *We Seven* by the Astronauts Themselves, Simon & Schuster 1962, from the chapter by Wally Schirra, Jr. "Some Séances in the Room," p 116.

I was very relieved that someone as calm and thorough—and stubborn—as Deke Slayton was worrying about the Atlas. I have often thought—suppose I am laying up there on top of that thing, ready to blast off. And I'm getting a little vibration that I have not expected.. The Atlas down below me is banging and whining, and I'm worried that maybe it's going to spoil my day. I can call Slayton on the radio and say "Hey, Deke, what's all this shaking and rattling I'm getting here?"

Deke will have the instruments in front of him in the blockhouse, and he has studied the bird so well that he can come back and say, "I've noticed that myself, Wally. Don't worry about it. That's just the hootenanny valve on the whatchamacallit fluttering a little. I saw it do the same thing out at the Convair plant in San Diego. It doesn't mean a thing. Forget it."

That's all I would need to know. And maybe I could return the favor someday if Deke was up there and he did not like the way his oxygen system was working. Then it would be my turn to help."

From JOHN MEDINA, past GD Security Guard

WHO ARE YOU AGAIN?

On my first assignment at Sycamore Canyon Test Site, at the Assembly Building, I couldn't believe the size of the Atlas Missile on its side as big as a locomotive! I was on duty when a gentleman engaged me in conversation, asking me if it was my first day there. Someone from the stand where the missile was being worked on called to the man I was talking to, "Hey Charlie, we need you up here."

Charlie (Varnes) put his cup of coffee on my desk and went to attend to the problem on "the bird", then another worker (Russ Addy) approached me. He then left to get on the stand where the missile was being readied for its first static firing. As Russ Addy left my location he turned back and said, "Nice talking to you, Charlie." I was a bit confused. A few minutes later I got up to stretch my legs. When I walked around I noticed the coffee cup had a name on it; the name was "Charlie", who I learned was the supervisor on the missile crew that was called up to the stand. When he put his cup down facing away from me the name Charlie was on the cup.

My next assignment a couple of days later, was at the "Y (or 4) Point Security Check Point." Anyone on duty at the "Y" (or 4) had to check all badges and clearances, including the bus that brought the Mechanics, Techs and Engineers through there. On my first assignment at the "Y," I boarded the crew bus and who was the first guy up front? "Russ Addy." He greeted me with a "Good morning, Charlie." Immediately I became known as Charlie to fifteen workers. It took quite a while to get my name back. Sometimes someone at Site One would call out "Hey, Charlie." I wouldn't respond, someone else would say, "I think so-and-so is trying to get your attention."

One of our supervisors at Sycamore one night saw a small fire off in the distance from the admin building at Sycamore. He went to investigate. There was a guy with a small campfire, a pup tent and all the makings of a camp. Lieutenant Aguilar asked the guy what he was doing. He said "I'm camping."

Aguilar said, "This is private land (Air Force). You can't do that here."

The camper responded, "Well the sign at the entrance said **Cleveland National Forest** so that's why I'm camping here." He was allowed to spend the night.

From MEL JONES

The Night Hurricane Donna Visited Cape Canaveral

September always reminds me of the same month in 1960 when Hurricane Donna blew by Cape Canaveral on a Friday night. Donna was forecast to bring strong hurricane force winds and considerable damage, so all Cape activities were shut down, launch areas buttoned-up and rockets returned to their hangars. This was two months after I joined Convair Astronautics at the Cape as the electrical engineer in Plant Engineering Department 571-7.

Being the new, young guy, I was tasked to pull Hurricane Watch Duty that Friday along with co-workers Bob and Charlie. I never did learn what Bob and Charlie had done wrong to deserve this special duty with me. Anyway, we three were to remain overnight in our small Plant Engineering office off ICBM Road just in case something might happen during the storm at any of our four Atlas Launch Complexes and two Main Hangars. There was absolutely nothing we could have done about anything, but nevertheless Chuck, the Plant Engineering Manager, insisted we had to be there.

Except for a few Security Police and the three of us, all other Cape personnel had been evacuated and most all facilities throughout the Cape were secured and powered down.

Late that Friday afternoon Donna's rain and wind kicked-up and rapidly grew stronger after dark. Fortunately, our small building still had phone service and electricity and so we hunkered down with a deck of cards and a big pot of coffee to help us ride-out the storm and get through the night. Inside our old, but sturdy, office building we felt safe and comfortable and were glad we didn't have to venture out anywhere.

Around two a.m., I briefly checked conditions outside and encountered drenching, stinging rain then blowing sideways in the pitch black dark. Donna's fury was peaking about three a.m. when the office phone rang and was answered by Bob, who nodded my way and said, "He wants to speak with you."

I asked who it was and Bob replied, "It's Chuck. And he wants to speak with you right now." Chuck was calling from his home in Cocoa Beach and had apparently prepared for the hurricane in his own way by enjoying entirely too much good scotch. His speech was somewhat slurred but he informed me that I was to go out right away and inspect all Atlas Complexes and Hangars, and report back to him as soon as possible.. I reminded Chuck how bad conditions had gotten outside and asked why it was so important that I go out then to check on things. Chuck emphasized it was necessary in case he were to get a phone call from the "Old Man" (Convair Base Manager B.G. McNabb). If the "Old Man" should call, Chuck needed to know what to tell him.

McNabb had a particular interest in our Launch Complex-14 which was then being adapted for the Mercury Astronaut Program. Realizing it would be pointless to argue with Chuck, I agreed to go, and hung up the phone. I told Bob and Charlie what Chuck wanted and said I was first going to enjoy another cup of coffee and hoped the storm might soon slack off. A bit later I donned rain gear and went out to make my rounds as Chuck had ordered.

All entrance gates had been chained and padlocked by Security Police so access beyond each area's guard post wasn't possible unless you had a key. I didn't have one and wasn't about to ask Security Police to come and unlock a gate during the storm. But to keep my word to Chuck, I dutifully drove around to all our areas and used my car's headlights to peer as best I could into the darkness beyond the gates. I could faintly make out both Hangars as well as the Test Stands and Service Towers at our Launch Complexes. All appeared intact as were the well-fortified Blockhouses.

The only things I could personally inspect were the Ready Rooms located just outside each Complex gate; and they appeared OK save for a few small pieces of blown-off siding. The Ready Room buildings were less sturdy than anything else, and so I concluded all other of our facilities must have experienced very little, if any, damage. This turned out to be the case.

After one-and-one-half hours of slowly making my rounds, I was thoroughly drenched and also disgusted with the thought of being the only human roaming around the Cape in such deplorable conditions. So, on my way back to the office I came up with an idea of what to tell Chuck as a kind of payback for him giving me such an unpleasant assignment. I told Bob and Charlie of my findings and they wanted to know what I planned to report. I didn't tell them all that I had in mind but said they could listen in on my call. Until then, I expected to unwind with some hot coffee and dry out.

A little after five a.m. I phoned Chuck at his home. It seemed like his phone rang forever but was finally picked up and then immediately dropped, banging around a few times on the floor. Chuck got on the phone, and answered with a very slow, slurred, response, "Huuuuh?" It was apparent he had been aroused from a very deep sleep, probably scotch-induced.

Several times I mentioned who I was but it didn't seem to register and he kept asking my name and why was I calling? After a few attempts, he eventually understood who I was but still wondered why I called. I reminded him of his instruction for me to let him know the condition of all our Convair areas in case Base Manager McNabb called him for a report. As Chuck began to recollect, I urged him to get a good grip on himself before I continued with the news.

Once he was ready, I went on to explain that it might be hard to believe, but the Mercury-Atlas Service Tower on Launch Complex 14 had been blown over and completely destroyed. There was then a long pause of complete silence by Chuck, quickly followed by a string of nasty expletives ending with his repeated exclamation, "Oh No! Oh No! How am I ever going to tell McNabb about this."

I tried to regain Chuck's attention, and when he finally stopped to catch his breath, I called out, "Chuck! Chuck! Calm down. I wasn't serious, just kidding. As far as I can tell, everything's OK—including the Complex 14 Service Tower."

Another moment of silence ensued on Chuck's end and then I heard a loud, "Aw, sh*t!!" as he slammed down the phone without another word. Bob and Charlie had listened to the whole conversation and were absolutely convinced I made Chuck furious and was sure to be in big trouble with him when everyone got back together on Monday. They feared they might also feel Chuck's wrath by association with me—and even speculated we all might be fired.

Monday came soon enough and most all Convair activities resumed along with necessary post-hurricane clean-up. At Plant Engineering, word had spread about my phone call with Chuck during the storm and all eyes were on me expectantly as Chuck arrived late for work and assumed his place at his desk perched on a raised platform in the middle of the room.

We awaited an outburst from him at any moment and were astonished that he never said word one that whole day, or later, about my phony report. He seemed to carry on as if nothing upsetting had happened the last few days except for Donna's winds and rain, about which he dictated a favorable condition report to San Diego headquarters. The rest of us agreed to avoid any mention to Chuck about the matter.

Later on, those of us who knew the whole story were able to joke and laugh about it, finally realizing Chuck had obviously been too intoxicated to ever recall my trumped-up report about the blown-over Service Tower. Fortunately, Chuck's recall malfunction gave us safe cover and turned out to be the only thing to inject some much needed levity into the memory of what we had experienced on the night Hurricane Donna visited Cape Canaveral.

FROM KAY QUIJADA

HERE'S A LITTLE "GOTCHA" STORY FOR YA.

It was the 1960s era at Kearny Mesa's Astronautics. I was a young clerk working in the Engineering Release Group on the second shift. Our supervisor was a fellow that fancied himself as a ladies man, a Clark Gable. This supervisor always brought a large thermos bottle with his own special coffee that was "you bet—better than coffee machine" and seemed to have nothing to do but watch the rest of us work while sipping coffee at his leisure.

One evening, someone secretly exchanged some of the coffee in his thermos with sour pickle juice. Out of the corners of our eyes, we discretely watched as he relaxed, leaning back in his cushioned supervisor's chair and filled his coffee cup. Then, much to our delight, he took a drink, promptly spewed out the doctored coffee all over his desk, jumped out of his chair and yelled "What the Hxxx!" We all felt enormously gratified by his unhappy discomfort. Of course, we all acted surprised and unknowing of who would do such a dastardly prank!

FROM TOM LEECH, KEARNY MESA VIBRATION TEST LAB, ABOUT '60-'61

VISITORS HAVE DIFFERENT FORMS

We were a high profile company and project in the early sixties. We had visitors constantly coming in—we usually knew from the posters placed all around the plant—to see what we were up to. Politicians, generals, you name it. However, the one who created the biggest stir out in my corner of the plant, the Test Labs, was from a visitor who was appearing in a musical across the street at Circle Arts Theater. When Juliet Prowse strolled with her escort past our Test Lab area,

Juliet Prowse in 1960. Courtesy Wikipedia

the whole gang took an impromptu break to check her out, discretely, of course.

FROM ED BOCK. 1961, VANDENBERG AFB. ATLAS PROGRAM FIELD OPERATIONS

REMEMBER "THE GREEN HORNET?"

I joined GD in June 1961 fresh out of college. I was hired into the Atlas Silo Missile Lift System GSE (Ground Support Equipment) group led by Russ Thomas. After several months of orientation, I was sent to Vandenberg's OSTF Two (Operational System Test Facility, maybe) to learn about the Atlas F silo. The plan was to get me familiar enough so I could do GSE Tiger Team duty on the operational sites throughout the United States.

Conditions at Vandenberg AFB were primitive; shared hotel rooms and no rental cars. GD's Vandenberg base operations also didn't have any cars for young whipper snapper associate engineers from San Diego. I reported to OSTF Two by bus and was promptly put to work writing Engineering Change Notices to document such things as wrong size holes, misplaced brackets.

After several weeks of this, I decided that I wasn't learning much about the silo. The folks that were really involved with big picture issues were the American Machine and Foundry (AMF) field reps at the site; most of the missile lift equipment in the silo was supplied by AMF. This AMF team was working under a subcontract managed by my boss, Russ Thomas.

One morning, I walked out to the AMF trailer and introduced myself to Lew Fowler, the leader of the AMF field team. He welcomed me and said I could work with his team. Since I didn't have a car, he offered me use of the Green Hornet, a beat up puke green Ford sedan with a faded AMF meatball on the side. Life was wonderful!!! What I didn't know until later was that Lew had been trying to convince Russ that he needed to lease a better car.

Once I started using the Green Hornet, Lew leased a new car for the AMF Team. When Russ found out what had happened, he was somewhat displeased. I did learn a great deal about the silo working with the AMF guys, and later used that knowledge in visits to about half of the operational Atlas silos.

FROM TOM LEECH, TEST LABS KEARNY MESA

ALL WORK AND DEFINITELY SOME PLAY

Our inter-departmental athletic teams worked on a joint effort by day and battled on the court or diamond at night (or vice versa as Astro was going full bore with multiple shifts much of the time.) My Test Labs basketball team included several players who'd done well on their own college teams, and other teams were equally well-stocked.

Astro had a women's team that competed in the inter-company league. They challenged our men's team to a game so we assembled at Balboa Park Muni Gym for the event. Generally we had few spectators, but for this one, the spouses decided to show up en masse. We had a much more enjoyable game than when playing against the maintenance or computer teams, and with all those watchful eyes on us, it was probably one of our cleanest games. I don't recall who won, which was immaterial. (A colleague will remember this, right Donna?)

REMEMBER WHEN WE WERE ALL COEDS?

Back around 1960, when I was at the Kearny Mesa Building Four as part of the Test Lab crew, Astro division management decided to check the troops' working efficiency. One feature was to send several snoopers around to observe how hard, or in what manner, we were working away. A tricky aspect was when they observed an engineer, or anyone, not diligently toiling away with a manual or slide rule (I realize younger folks won't know what that gadget is), but were looking into the air or perhaps out a window (if they had one near). Was that person day-dreaming, snoozing, or perhaps thinking about some work aspect? If they felt it was the latter, e.g., mentally thinking about work, they came up with the initialism C-O-E-D. So were we males (and females of course) being labeled as "coeds?" Hmmm...Well, that was explained to us as meaning that person was likely not goofing off, but **Concentrating On Engineering Design.** Somehow we all got pretty good at that, once we discovered what kind of staring look would qualify us as a COED.

Faber-Castell Slide Rule from Wikipedia By Gisling - Own work

FROM JOHN MEDINA, GD SECURITY

MORNIN' ASTRONAUTS

Ray Blair would frequently bring visitors and dignitaries to Sycamore Canyon Test Site on a company bus. We were always notified of such visits. One morning the bus pulled up to the administration building. Ray stepped off the bus and the seven original astronauts stepped off to come into the building. What a momentous event! John Glenn, Gus Grissom and the rest.

They passed out lapel pins with their names on the pins! I happened to get two pins and gave them away to a cousin's son who was in grade school. His bedroom looked like outer space and no space; he collected everything he could. He wanted me to get him any papers that had anything to do with missiles and space. From Ken Newton, I got the used countdown sheet of one of the test firings and sent it to him.

FROM TOM LEECH

From my 1997 SD Magazine article "When Aerospace Was King: a former employee offers an insider's reflections on the heyday of GD in San Diego."

WHAT'S THAT ABOUT TURTLES? IN SPACE???

In February 1962, John Glenn became the first American to orbit the earth, lifted there by an Atlas Booster. Scott Carpenter, Wally Schirra and Gordon Cooper followed, making 100% program success. Advance to 1997, to a Coronado book signing by the three Navy pilots, all San Diego residents and authors of *From Wildcat to Tomcat*. One of them was Wally Schirra. After hearing about my having worked on the Mercury Atlas program, he signed my copy **"Thanks for the lift—it was <u>not</u> a blast**."

THE TURTLE GAME

Humor was a frequent part of that world; perhaps because so many people were young, the paychecks good, the programs exciting. Jokes and stories would move quickly through the many Kearny Mesa buildings or in and out from the launch ranges and other facilities. Some of it was pretty stupid; such as the turtle game. The idea was to ask someone, usually in a somewhat public arena, "Are you a turtle?" That person had to answer "You bet your sweet ass I am," or buy a round of drinks. Even somewhat mature vice-presidents and program directors would spring that on each other at a time such that to give the answer would be embarrassing for the responder (a simpler era).

The aforementioned Schirra, designated High Potentate of Turtles, was reporting live from orbit on an Apollo mission, when he sprung the turtle question on fellow Mercury astronaut Deke Slayton, the ground-based controller. After some squirming, Slayton shut off the mike and stated the required answer, thus ducking buying the round for all listening. (As noted in *The Light Stuff*, by Bob Ward.) That phrase, slightly modified, became part of the national lingo via Rowan and Martin's Laugh In: "You bet your sweet bippy."

FROM JIM MEYER, SCIENTIFIC DIGITAL COMPUTER LAB, KEARNY MESA MERCURY PROGRAM ABOARD ATLAS

PLAN B IF NEEDED

Launch Complex 14 at Cape Canaveral ready to launch Friendship 7. Photo by NASA

When John Glenn's first Mercury mission occurred, all three major networks set up "news rooms" in Kearny Mesa Building Four across the hall from the digital computer lab, analog computer lab, and the telemetry data processing station. When the Mercury capsule flew over San Diego, the telemetry station would be collecting and recording data in real time. One of the most interesting items was Glenn's heartbeat. This would be displayed and shown live to the nation watching on TV.

After the mission was successful, we heard that the telemetry guys were prepared to display a recording of a chimpanzee's heartbeat if Glenn's was not received!

FROM ERIC HERZ

MORE ON JIM MEYER'S STORY ABOUT JOHN GLENN'S FLIGHT

I was the supervisor of the design and implementation section of the Telemetering Data Station and Carl Dragila was in charge of the whole complex. Senior engineer Dave Fyffe, who was in charge of maintenance and repair, "manufactured" and operated the roof antenna when Glenn flew overhead. We separated the Station in the middle by a black curtain—one side for NBC and the other for CBS. ABC came in to us too late. All the space was spoken for. Carl Dragila took charge of the NBC half and I had the CBS side.

We had been briefed about what we could not say on the air when we would be interviewed by the reporters who were in the Station during the whole flight—particularly what was forbidden for us to comment about was what do the telemetered signals signify about Glenn's health and were assured that the commentators knew not to ask us. The signals we displayed were electrocardiogram (EKG) and respiration.

Sure enough I was asked by the commentator what the EKG told me about Glenn. I was unprepared for that question and did not know what to say. I am sure it was edited out. By the way, we had the pulse signal of Enos, the first chimpanzee to achieve orbit, and all the other Astronauts during launch. Wally Schirra was the calmest. Jim's is a good story but I believe it is based on what our fellow engineers in the adjacent labs thought we were capable of doing rather than what we would actually do.

(More) That roof antenna that Dave Fyffe made did a lot of good in other ways. We could watch launches from Vandenberg once the missile rose above the horizon at about 55,000 feet. One time in the early sixties we captured the telemetry when Vandenberg had missed recording it, and another time when Al Mardel of Test Evaluation fame watched about a dozen signals that we displayed on strip chart recorders for him for only the first five seconds when they were visible yelled out "she is going to blow up." Nobody else could do that.

From JOHN GLENN

FAME MAY NOT BE WIDESPREAD

From *John Glenn: a Memoir,* by Col. John Glenn, USMC, page 280

After the welcome home ceremonies at that Cape and a news conference the next day in which I described my feeling at being inside the reentry fireball as "cautious apprehension," Annie, Dave, Lyn, and I spent the remainder of the weekend in seclusion on the naval base at Key West.

Having their company and no one else's for a change was a pleasure. We walked on the beach and swam, and I caught up on everything that had been going on at home and in school in the weeks leading up to the flight. But it wasn't a trip given entirely to leisure. The president had told me I had been invited to address a joint session of Congress the following Monday, after a parade in Washington.

I worked on my speech, and on Monday morning we flew to the airport at West Palm Beach to meet the president for the trip back to Washington on *Air Force One*. Jackie was going to be staying in Long Beach with Caroline and their infant son, John Jr. Jackie wanted Caroline to meet us, so they came out to the airport with the president to see us off.

We were on the plane, and the president boarded, and behind him came Jackie with little Caroline, holding her by the hand, and Jackie said, "Caroline, this is the astronaut went around the Earth in the spaceship. This is Colonel Glenn."

Caroline looked at me, and then all around the plane. Finally she turned back to me, her face disappointed, and said in a quavering voice, "But where's the monkey?"

FROM BOB VOTH

ANOTHER MERCURY TALE...A CLASSIC LINE...MERCURY NERVOUSNESS?

During the middle of the Mercury Program (Atlas Launches of the astronauts into space) several of the original seven astronauts were visiting the Astronautics Division to review the progress on the next launch vehicle. We were gathered around a drafting table in the mechanical engineering area. Charlie Pruckner asked them "How does it feel to be launched into space?"

I believe it was Gordon Cooper who answered "It is a bit disconcerting to know you are riding on low-bid hardware."

FROM DON SULLIVAN

BACK WHEN IT TOOK MORE THAN "COOKIES" TO MOVE THOSE SOVIETS

During the Cuban Missile Crisis, we were directed to arm all of the Atlas missiles that were available with live warheads and be prepared to launch if directed by President Kennedy. We had not turned any of the operational units over to the Air Force, but they provided one officer to be prepared to press the launch button at each site. We had fifteen missiles ready at Cheyenne, Wyoming and nine more at Omaha, Nebraska. There were also a few at Vandenberg and Florida.

President Kennedy made it clear that if the Russians did not turn around and go home, we would be forced to launch at their country. During that time, we were directed to remain at the launch pads around the clock.

Each missile pad had a large status board in the blockhouse that provided the green lights that represented every system affecting the missile. As long as all lights were green, the launch button remained green. After about the first four hours, one of the missiles at Cheyenne developed a red light that indicated that a "missile on stand" switch had a problem. That red light had to be fixed or the missile could not be launched.

The responsibility for the system that controlled the light was mine. The switch was located on the Erection Mechanism Nose Clamp near the warhead. I was known as the "Erection Mechanism Expert" and lived with that name even though I got teased from time to time. I immediately had the blast doors of the blockhouse to be opened and I ran to the missile to check it out. Access to the switch could only be reached by placing a ladder near the warhead and straddling same. I was shocked to find that the switch was way out of adjustment and could not turn the green light on in the blockhouse. Since I had set all the switches for every missile at Cheyenne, I was dumbfounded.

FUN ON THE JOB

Suddenly I realized what had caused the problem. The nose clamp on the horizontal boom had a thick pad which the front of the missile had compressed more due to the added weight of the live warhead. I quickly made the rounds of all the missiles advising those in Omaha to do the same and readjust the switch. Needless to say, the fact that I had been straddling a live nuclear warhead will remain with me for the rest of my life!

FROM PHIL BUNCH

ALWAYS GOOD TO CHECK THE OIL

From Atlas Recollections—Atlas 50th book 1957-2007, page 55.

Early August 1962, I was preparing to leave Site Four on my way to Roswell, New Mexico and I was asked to close the Silo doors. If the doors were left open awhile the hydraulic oil tended to drain back into the reservoir, so here I was standing on the silo cap and gave the word to close the doors. Well they went into free fall till hitting the oil remaining in the cylinder. Scared the**** out of me. Just one of many scary incidents on site.

FROM CALVIN FOWLER

MERCURY NERVOUS TIMES, AND PEOPLE

I was the Mercury Atlas Test Conductor on Pad Fourteen for Carpenter (Mercury-Atlas-7), Schirra (MA-8) and Cooper (MA-9). As we were preparing for Schirra's flight, his parents lived about five miles from the plant in San Diego. They started calling the plant every day with questions about their son (Wally Schirra). Finally GD Astro in San Diego decided I should come to San Diego and visit with Wally's parents.

I left Patrick Air Force Base (PAFB) in Florida on Saturday morning on a DC-6 freight airplane and got to San Diego around six p.m. Saturday afternoon. The company had a car for me at the airport and a motel room in Mission Valley. Sunday I got up and ate breakfast at the motel. I called Wally's parents and told them who I was and they invited me to their house. We talked for a while, then Mrs. Schirra served lunch for the three of us.

In the afternoon as we were talking, Wally Sr. asked if I wanted a drink. He served me a couple Scotch and waters. Finally, about five p.m. I went back to the airport and got on the DC-6 for the flight back to Patrick AFB in Florida. We arrived about eight-thirty in the morning. I got into my car and reported to Pad 14 around nine a.m.

From that day on Wally's parents never called the plant worrying about Wally. I did go to see them every time I was in San Diego after that trip. I even had to assure them Wally was safe on his Gemini flight.

FROM DON GIEGLER

REPRODUCING CONSISTENT SOLUTIONS TOOK SPECIAL SKILLS

From Atlas Recollections—Atlas 50th book 1957-2007

In the early 1960s, Atlas and Centaur autopilot dynamics was determined with the help of analog computer simulation of vehicle rigid body and propellant sloshing modes. Because the analog computer simulations relied on networks of operational amplifiers subject to noise and drift, difficulty in obtaining consistent solutions for the same set of equations with the same initial conditions was often encountered.

One day a colleague, who was trying to obtain such solutions, leaned back on his chair in front of an analog computer console and exclaimed, "This darned machine won't reproduce!"

An older colleague from the same branch walked by and, without cracking a smile, instructed, "Remove the contraceptive."

A major function of the branch was determination of autopilot gains for stable vehicle dynamics over various flight phases. Dr. Al Schmitt had a cigar box/dart arrangement he used to ward off those pressing him too hard for these gains. Al, the branch manager at the time, had written possible gains on scraps of paper he kept in the cigar box. Under pressure from a zealous project or program manager, he would place the open box on the floor, some distance from his desk and launch darts into the box interior. The first candidate he skewered from each of the three sets of scraps were offered to the requestor as the preliminary numbers. Time to determine the final settings was generally not a problem after these sessions.

From BOB FOLEY

To hire or not to hire, is that even a question?

An improbable (but true) story about my first job. Some names have been changed to avoid embarrassing innocent bystanders and others.

In the spring of 1962, I was a struggling Engineering Science major at Pratt Institute in Brooklyn, New York. I had made it through the first three years of a four year Bachelor of Science program. but Advanced Calculus and other math laden classes threatened to wash me out, I was not a good student and I was lonely and worried and. discouraged. I knew that I should be going on interview trips and seeking employment but my heart was not in it. I was beginning to wonder if I had made a big mistake. There were twelve seniors in the department and I was usually eleventh in GPA.

Also on my mind was the mandatory-for-graduation Senior Project. Each student was supposed to write a proposal disclosing the subject, scope and lab equipment needed. The proposal would be reviewed by the department chairman, a Dr. Published (real name withheld), who had authored a series of advanced textbooks on dynamics of solids, fluids and gases. If the department chairman didn't approve your proposal, he would assign you a subject to be investigated.

I decided to go for the chairman's choice route, so I wrote a brief proposal asking for approval of a project in the area of solid fuel rockets. As I expected, the answer was 'NO'. I believe it's called "gaming the system." I was summoned to Dr. Published's office where, in a brief meeting, I learned my project would involve digital computers and my adviser would be a young Ph.D., Dr. Pshaw.

I went directly to Dr. Pshaw's office. He was busy and tried to send me away. I told him that Dr. Published had sent me and I would be asking his advice. Did we (Pratt) have a digital computer? No. But we were obtaining one! He took me upstairs to the future computer room. It was empty except for three or four equipment cabinets and a shelf with a few manuals from the Itty Bitty Machine Co. (an informal iteration of International Business Machines or IBM) Further investigation revealed the fact that the cabinets housed an IBM 1620 computer...it just hadn't been installed yet. Dr. Pshaw showed me the input devices—a console typewriter and paper tape reader and punch—told me to report problems and progress weekly, and walked away.

I dug into the manuals. In the next couple of weeks I learned the basics: what was a 1620 stored program computer and what a stored program computer could do and what were the differences between a decimal computer and a binary(or octal) computer. I also got acquainted with FORTRAN and GOTRAN and learned enough about 1620 machine language to enter a "Bootstrap" to accept records from the console typewriter and punch them on the paper tape punch (a real bottleneck), and another to read paper tape into memory and then execute what was read in.

Soon I got a "shopping list" of utility programs that Dr. Pshaw and/or the grad students wanted or needed. Prominent on the list was the demand for a robust Polynomial Solver. I implemented Cardan's Method and Brown's Method and hoped that would keep them busy for a while. I quickly became the local computer nerd. I started boning up on iterative techniques and often signed up for the five to six p.m. "slot" and stayed until ten p.m. or later.

With the finish line in sight, I perked up and sent out a few job applications I was still behind in my studies so I declined most invitations to travel for interviews. I received three or four offers, almost all for jobs on the East Coast and with no commitment to let me work in their programming sections. All the offers were within a few dollars of each other (per month). All I wanted was to move to the West Coast and be allowed to write programs for a big, fast computer.

One company, General Dynamics Astronautics, sent an engineer to Brooklyn to interview me. This turned into something of a fiasco when it developed that the interviewer was more interested in finding an open tavern than interviewing me. The guy was on Layoff status: he had been given the choice of taking a Reduction in Force (RIF) immediately or doing two weeks on travel, interviewing applicants and then, being laid off (RIFed). He handed me an employment application form and we parted. I returned to my rented room and tossed the application form on the IWNH ("It Will Never Happen") pile.

Graduation Day was June 11—final grades would be posted soon. I got an A for my Senior Project. Then Western Union brought a telegram to my door (I had no telephone). The telegram was from General Dynamics in San Diego...very apologetic...it said they had misplaced my application and would I submit another one? I decided to apply. Graduation Day was June 11th. What the heck? I did apply and the folks at GD Astronautics sent me an offer that I quickly accepted. I drove to San Diego and went to work on June 25, 1962.

FROM BILL CHANA

An item from his book *Over the Wing: the Bill Chana Story*, page 129. Used with permission

CRITTERS CAUSING TROUBLE AT SYCAMORE

In late 1962, Bill became the Base Manager at the Sycamore Canyon Test Site. GD bought the acreage north of the Sycamore test site. Since the Sycamore site was government property, GD could now develop sites on its own property. Roads leading to a number of small test pads were graded. A small building was erected on the property to produce a ship launched missile developed by the GD Pomona division. Chuck Graser, my Operations Chief, later became the manager of this facility.

The snakes and wild animals that made their home in Sycamore Canyon interfered to some extent with our operations. Each of our block houses had a hard-line telephone connection to observation posts that were manned during hot firing tests. The observers, using high-powered binoculars, could alert the test conductor in the block house if anything unusual was occurring at the test stand. We regularly had to repair the communications cables that ran between these observation posts and the block house. The lines often were severed in several places as if cut by a pair of sharp shears. There was some suspicion that the deer in the area were tripping over the lines.

We called any wildlife expert who diagnosed the problem immediately. He said, "If you will raise the communication cables about two feet above the ground your troubles will be over. Deer can easily jump over a cable but when they see it lying on the ground they think it is a snake and will stomp on it until they think it has been killed, i.e., when the cable is severed. We raised the cables as suggested and never had that problem again.

Rattlesnakes were plentiful in Sycamore Canyon. Our security and firefighting teams became experts at capturing them. We had rattlesnake skins hanging in the fire house that were four to six feet long. We were to call security immediately if one of those critters came wandering into the work areas.

FROM TED LAMOUREUX

IF ROCKETS ARE OK, WHY NOT CANNONS?

From his *My Life at Convair*, p16.

As I said before it was not all work and no play. The company was continually updating our vibration capability and they installed a signal generator to sweep through our 2-2000Hz frequency range. It was done automatically and all the operator had to do was control the signal voltage to achieve the desired G (force) level. The system was run by a tape with a preset frequency change for the desired test time.

One night one of the guys asked me if he brought in a tape with music on it could we run the music through the vibration exciter? Since the exciter was an over grown speaker I told him we could try it during our lunch break. Several days later he brought in a tape of the 1812 Overture. At lunch we set it up and keeping the "G" level low we tried it. The music came through nice and clear, especially the cannons. We decided to try it with more volume. We turned it on and went outside to listen to it through our metal building. We had adjusted the volume to prevent damage to the equipment.

When the cannons were fired the noise was loud enough to bring the guards from the adjacent guard shack running over to where we were gathered. Well they wanted us to play it again and we asked them not to tell anyone because it was unauthorized use of the equipment. It was kept secret and then we found out we weren't the only ones trying to determine the capability of the equipment.

From TOM HETER

Ultra-scientific launch techniques

I remember a launch at Complex ABRES (Advanced Ballistic Re-Entry Systems) at Vandenberg Air Force Base in the early days. I was a red line monitor for an Atlas launch. We were in the final minute and someone came on the net and said "ABORT" as the battery voltage was zero. The response from Ken Hankins, the test conductor, was "HORSE SHIT! IT CAN'T BE!!!!!!!!!" And the Atlas lit up and flew a successful flight launch to the Marshal Islands. The Air Force Colonel. in charge of the launch was Bobby Houchins and he just laughed and said "That is a Launch Conductor that knows his STUFF!!!!!!!!!!"

General Quarters

I was the Launch Conductor for 39E/NOAA F—a National Oceanic and Atmospheric Administration (NOAA) Weather Satellite. We were in December trying to launch. I had 13 launch attempts that were scrubbed and we flew on the fourteenth try. I had a quarter that I flipped each attempt and it came up tails. On the fourteenth try it came up heads and I told the team this is the DAY and we flew a successful mission. Guess what happened to the quarter. I SPENT IT!!!!!!

As a side I had the only Commit Stop that we had in years during the attempts. It was a guidance failure from the General Electric guidance station at about T-minus-20 sec. We tried another day and all was OK!!!!

From CHUCK ADKISON, NASA San Diego Resident Office

Is this man a bad luck symbol?

Shortly after the NASA Lewis Research Center took over the Atlas-Centaur(AC) Program from The NASA Marshall Space Flight Center there was a launch failure (AC-3 or 4, around 1963). The new NASA managers traveled to San Diego for a failure analysis presentation by Deane Davis, who headed the Astro Upper Stage Program Office. Deane opened his presentation with a projection showing an alligator in a swamp and followed that by stating; **"It is very diffi-**

cult to remember that your objective was to drain the swamp when you are up to your ass in alligators!" Not one person laughed as I remember.

Fast forward a couple decades. Even though I had been on the Atlas-Centaur Program since its inception I had never attended a launch. Larry Ross had just been promoted as Director of the Lewis Research Center when I got my chance to attend the AC-43 launch. For those of you that remember, AC-43 was a spectacular failure. Larry Ross immediately assembled the NASA launch team in the Architect and Engineering (A&E) building to review the details. Larry's opening question was; who is here that has never attended a launch before. I raised my hand and Larry said; "Chuck, don't ever come back!"

From JACK WRIGHT

Early Murphy's Law Centaur Interference

In looking at the Centaur history data, I see not the launch I observed in the June, 1963-April, 1965 timeframe. I arrived at the cape in June 63, representing Honeywell, to check out and calibrate the first IGS to guide a spacecraft into orbit.

The first launch got off the pad about 10 feet, failed one engine and dropped back into the pad. The result was a whiteout and small pieces scattered everywhere. I'm not sure if there was a test launch before that.

*A **plugs-out test** deter-mines whether the space-craft would operate nomi-nally on (simulated) internal power while detached from all cables and umbilicals.*

We had not installed the optical theodolite on the pad yet, to con-trol the drift in the platform. I calibrated the first Inertial Guid-ance System in the lab which was then moved to the vehicle, and we calibrated it again on the pad. We went thru a plugs-out, then a tanking test. We took advantage of that to get data with the cold stuff loaded.

Following that the Librascope computer failed and we decided to change just that component instead of the whole backups IGS. A peculiar thing happened. That computer had a defective relay that switched from ground power to airborne power. That was tested, we thought, in our setup in the lab, but in retrospect we realized it was not. On that first launch, the engine failed but our computer went into stop at power switch. Honeywell was lucky?

The one thing that would have been caught in a plugs-out test, was bypassed. Example of Murphy's law. It forced us to rethink our (GD's) lab hookup.

The second launch was successful and beforehand, STL (Space Technology Laboratories, a division of Thompson Ramo Wooldridge Inc., better known as TRW) asked if there was any-thing to be gained by keeping up the tracking data. My answer was "just the temperature data" (ha). We needed that to see the real ef-fects in space, and subsequently Honeywell recalculated the heat transmission and painted the gold plating to white.

I don't know if Honeywell continued their systems or not, on the Centaur, but there were several flaws we caught in the GD lab be-fore launch. I went to IBM Saturn V in April, 65, eventually to John-son Space Center with TRW.

From Jack Gage

Shift change—Good bye

From the set of stories in Celebrating 50 Years of Atlas Success and the People Who Made It Possible

The Air Force was running a test on the missile and silo. They were lowering the big concrete doors on the top of the silo. They failed to raise the pressure on the hydraulic cylinders. Weighing many tons, the doors slammed shut showering the missile with pieces of concrete. The Air Force didn't want to remove the missile until the tests were completed.

Russell Meredith of Northrop Aircraft perfected the process of the **Heliarc weld** *in 1941. Meredith named the process Heliarc because it used a tungsten electrode arc and helium as a shielding gas, but it is often referred to as tungsten inert gas welding (TIG).*

Because of the amount of damage, they notified San Diego. I was sent out with a welder, George Rauche, to evaluate the damage and notify San Diego on what was needed to make the repairs. I was lowered inside the tank as the outside was very dirty making it hard to see any damage, but all the dents could be seen on the inside. We received the necessary materials from San Diego and had them lower us down to make the first repair. After the patch was made, we attempted to heliarc weld. In doing so, the dolly we were on would swing away.

We notified top side of our problem and they suggested that we be tied around the missile so we could weld. That worked fine, but created another problem. The pressure in the tank had to be lowered so we wouldn't blow a hole in it. That worked fine, but then the whistle blew for the workers to go home and they did. We did a lot of yelling and after quite a while someone came and asked what was wrong. We explained we were tied to the tank and would someone come down and untie us.

They took one look down and asked, "Who did that?" **No way were any of them coming down to untie us.** They did throw us a knife and said, "Cut yourself loose," which we did and then we lowered the dolly down to the bottom of the silo. After the repairs were completed, the Air Force was able to complete the test. (When we started the mock-up of the missile at Plant 1, Building 3, the main aisles that crossed in our area were affectionately called Hollywood and Vine.)

From ROBERT C. RISLEY, Location, the Cape, later Propulsion/Fluid Systems Design, Kearney Mesa

Getting those Atlases up back then, not an easy task

I remember Karl Kachigan's lucky sports coat, which he had to wear for every Atlas-Centaur launch. Most of the Tiger Team went to Hanger H during the final stages of the launch countdown and listened to the count on loudspeaker. The last few minutes before launch we would climb the ladder to the roof to see the liftoff—at least some of us younger ones did. What an experience to see the culmination of everyone's efforts and teamwork!

Those were exciting times. When there was a launch success, post-launch parties, thrown by the marketing department in a Cocoa Beach motel room were standard fare. Failed missions were a huge disappointment to all team members, regardless of the cause. Everyone was anxious to pitch in and do their parts in the failure investigation. The camaraderie in the program will never be forgotten.

From BILL HAIRE, Guidance Analysis, Kearny Mesa

Lots of action at Vandenberg

In the early sixties, when sent to Vandenberg Air Force Base to support Atlas-Agena space launches, we stayed in Santa Maria and transportation was supplied via company taxi to and from Vandenberg, which ran twice a day (once early in the morning and again in the evening). On one occasion, Jim Johnson and I were supporting an early morning launch which was scrubbed. Returning to the GD compound (via way of either GE or Burroughs personal since we didn't have our own transportation) we were informed that we would have to wait around for the rest of the day until the evening taxi to Santa Maria came by.

After wandering around, or sitting on our brief cases all day, when the taxi finally arrived we were informed that it was already full and it could only take one of us. This infuriated Jim, to the point that he told the driver that they would make room for the both of us since we had been waiting all day, or he would kick the driver out and he would drive the taxi. The taxi was a station wagon, and finally one of us (I can't remember which) was allowed to lay down in the back for the long ride back to Santa Maria.

In the sixties, on trips to support Ground Guidance Station Atlas-Agena space launches, transportation to Vandenberg was via the company King Air, and ground transportation was via company or Air Force-supplied taxi around or off the base. One time when supporting a launch, I flew up with Grant Hansen on board. When we got there he was greeted of course with base personnel with a car for him and his troops to use. When loading up, he noticed that I wasn't going with them and asked where I was going. I told him to take me to the Ground Guidance station via the base taxi service. He told the GD base personnel that had brought him a car, to give me one since the Guidance Station was so remotely located, which they did. Any time after that when someone from our group was

96

going to Vandenberg, I would call up the GD base guy (I can't remember who) who gave me the car for me and our support personnel.

FROM ART IMDIEKE, TEST EVALUATION

A-OK OR MAYBE NOT – OV1 AND TOMAHAWK DILEMMAS. FIRST DO YOU RECALL WHAT AN OV1 WAS? ANSWER LATER

Orbiting Vehicle or OV, originally designated **SATAR**, was a series of <u>American</u> <u>satellites</u> operated by the <u>US Air Force</u>, launched between 1965 and 1971. Forty seven satellites were built, of which forty three were launched and thirty seven reached <u>orbit</u>. Convair built the first series designated OV1.
Courtesy Wikipedia

OV1's 13 and 14 were successfully placed into orbit, most probably in 1967 (I don't remember exactly). I and Ed Horbett, a design engineer (primarily of the command system on the program) went to Cape Canaveral to analyze telemetry data to determine the health of the satellites. Although the launch was from Vandenberg AFB, control while in orbit was centered at the Cape. Data from the various ground stations was relayed there.

On our first contact, we looked at data from OV1-13. Everything appeared to be in perfect order. Then suddenly all measurements, though staying within their expected ranges, shifted slightly. What the hell was this? After scratching our heads for a while, Horbett came up with a good idea. He said, "Let's look at the satellite clock." Each satellite was equipped with an elapsed-time clock which was activated whenever the satellite was powered up. The time wasn't right for OV1-13 but did look right for OV1-14. After some time and a few phone calls we learned that the ground station at Point Mugu, California while testing its command system had inadvertently shut down 13 and turned on 14. The basic health measurements utilized the same locations in the telemetry bitstream on all OV1's so everything then made sense.

After another day, Ed returned to San Diego. I decided to stay one more day to make a final health check. Everything seemed normal on both satellites until I checked the spin rate on OV1-13 which was spin stabilized at a slow end-over-end spin rate. It had increased slightly. Now that appeared impossible. You might possibly make a case for a decreased rate but how could you explain an increase? I checked the data over and over again but kept coming up with the same result. Finally I called the Chief Engineer, Palmer Smith, and reported my findings. His response was not kind. He suggested that I may have had one too many the night before. But, I convinced him that I had been analyzing data for about 10 years now and figured I knew how.

Then other things began to happen. On successive contacts, data showed that the battery voltage was continuing to decrease. Experiments were cycled on and off to see if one of them was drawing too much current but that proved negative. The spin rate kept increasing slightly and the battery voltage decreasing. Eventually the voltage dropped below that required by the telemetry system and all data ceased. Radar data showed the satellite in its proper orbit but it was dead. I gathered as many of the data records as I could and returned to San Diego.

Back in San Diego we convened a failure investigation team which included a representative from Eagle Picher, the battery supplier. While never able to determine the cause with 100% certainty, we concluded it most probably went something like this: The battery over-charge protection circuitry had failed which had allowed the battery to over-charge and eventually blow a cell. This, and subsequent cell failures, accounted for the voltage reduction and would have produced a large amount of gas under the dome where the battery was located. Since the domes were not hermetically sealed, the gas found an escape route that aided the spin rate. (Note: My memory isn't that good and I may have OV1's 13 and 14 reversed).

May I digress from OV1 momentarily. The following occurred during Tomahawk testing. As a reward for their dedicated service on the program, a company plane-load (eight or nine) of secretaries was flown to Point Mugu to observe a ground launch (simulating a launch from a shipboard Armored Box Launcher), enjoy a nice lunch at the Officers Club and be flown back to San Diego. However, after they had arrived a heavy fog bank rolled in which caused the test to be delayed. A question arose as to whether the plane would even be able to return to pick up the girls or if they would have to remain overnight in the Point Mugu area.

Somebody came up with a great idea, I believe it was one of the secretaries. She suggested that all of the test team members from San Diego, who were all checked into a nice motel in Oxnard, throw their room keys in a pile on a table. Then each secretary would randomly select a key and stay the night with that room occupant. This would provide a roof over their heads on a chilly, foggy night. Of course the powers-that-be squelched that idea. Actually, the fog lifted somewhat, the plane was able to land and returned the girls to San Diego. I believe the next day, the secretaries were again flown to Point Mugu, observed a successful launch, enjoyed another nice lunch at the Officers Club and were flown back to San Diego.

OK, here's the answer. OV1 was a small satellite, built by GD Astro-Convair, and placed into orbit by Atlas. For full info visit http://astronautix.com/o/ov1.html. Another question: among lunchtime games played by San Diego troops were Peeknuckle and Yukor. How do you really spell both of those?

FROM TOM LEECH AS IT INVOLVES THE ABOVE COLLEAGUE. ALSO KEARNY MESA, GUIDANCE AND TRAJECTORY DESIGN

GOOD TO KEEP LEARNING

In the mid-sixties, we had some classes to enhance our technical smarts. This one, I believe about Kalman filters (whatever those are) was in a small room in our own area in Building Four, and held right after work (an important item). During the session I asked our

© Ron Leishman * www.ClipartOf.com/443683

learned instructor a question. Unfortunately during the answer I drifted off, mentally that is. Afterward I mentioned that to my fellow student-colleague, B.J. Haire. "These after work classes can be tough on the brain. I asked a question and went to sleep during the answer."

B.J.: "You asked a question?"

From BOB BUTTS, Centaur

ENGINEERS OFTEN SEE THINGS FROM DIFFERENT PERSPECTIVES

Early in the Centaur program two static test tanks were fabricated and dubbed the Battleship and Cruiser. They resembled the basic Centaur tank but were strictly non-flight. The Battleship was fabricated from one inch aluminum plate and the Cruiser from half inch. I believe their existence led to the following incident.

An engineer from the propulsion group contacted Dennis Murphy, a lead engineer in structural design, wanting to add provisions for a temperature or pressure transducer somewhere on the hydrogen tank wall. He had diligently calculated the exact location for the instrument and pointed it out to Dennis along with the comment that all that was required was to drill and tap a hole of the correct size at that spot. When Dennis asked him what he thought the tank wall thickness was his reply was, "About a half inch." When told that the actual wall thickness was 0.010" stainless steel he went off mumbling under his breath. To my knowledge no such instrumentation was ever added.

From GLEN WADLEIGH, Test Lab

BASE ACTIVATION—SERIOUS STUFF GETTING THOSE ATLASES UP

(PAY ATTENTION DON S)

When the bases were being activated, some concern existed as to the potential ground wind loads during erection of the vehicle, prior to lowering it into the silo. An associate test lab engineer and I were directed to pack up some instrumentation and go collect some data. The next scheduled erection was at Altus, Oklahoma. We were loaded onto the routine Off-Site transporter, the DC-3 Gooney bird. We novices were amazed to witness the bored Transportation Department guys hang their legs out the open side door of the cargo compartment while we cruised along at two or three thousand feet.

We arrived safely at the base and were told that (of course) the schedule had slipped and it would be after midnight before erection could resume. We headed for the night life of Altus. The best we could find was a high school roller skating rink set up on temporary plywood. We were welcomed and joined in till they folded at the ten o'clock curfew.

Of course the schedule had slipped some more but the manager told us to stand by. We found some silent concrete and cuddled up to the seventy-thousand pound?? silo doors and tried to sleep. When the sun came up we were told to pack up and go home without any data. He was the boss !

From BOB EIDSON

STORIES ABOUT "HOW WE GOT TO THE MOON."

Note: These are true and as Walker Cronkite said "This is as it Was and You Are There" (apologies to Walter) in his TV Show Intro!

During a visit to NASA's Marshall Space Flight Center to give the folks there an update on GD Testing of the Centaur (Cruiser Tank with Boost Pumps, Engine Feed System Ducting, Pressurization System and Vent Valves, etc.), I showed a film of the LH$_2$ (Liquid Hydrogen) Tank Interior which included Pressurization and Venting Cycles with the Pumps operating and around sixty percent Propellant Level. Vigorous Boiling of the LH$_2$ occurred during Venting! One of the Germans in the audience commented (German accent here) **"I do not understand ziz action!!"**

A voice from the audience, a chap name of Wernher Von Braun, responded **"Did You Effer Open a Can Of Hot Beer ???"**

From MARGARET "MAGGIE" LIMA

AH, THOSE MALE-FEMALE COMPLICATIONS AT THE CAPE

I hired in to General Dynamics here at the Cape in June of 1965, worked the entire time on the Atlas Program on Launch Complex 36A and B and retired from LC-41 with the Atlas V Program. I began as a Typist and retired as a Tech Writer, putting together the procedures used to check out and launch all the Atlas vehicles. During my tenure, I worked in Material, Site Engineering, Industrial Relations (now called HR) Data Analysis, Design Engineering, and Launch Operations.

Here are some of my personal humorous times at GD from days long past...like perhaps the time I asked to observe a launch from inside the blockhouse and was told NO, because there weren't facilities for a woman in the Blockhouse (that was remedied when we hired female engineers, some fifteen-plus years later and had to build restrooms at the Ramp and in the Blockhouse), and besides, the language sometimes gets a little rough for a lady, or...

The time I climbed into a dumpster to retrieve a hand-written letter my boss had given me to type for him. He said he put it on my desk, but I couldn't find it anywhere, and the janitor had come to pick up the trash. After thoroughly checking my desk and not finding it, I came to the conclusion that the only place it could be was in the trash that had just been dumped into the dumpster. So I soon discovered there wasn't a step on the inside of the dumpster, like there was on the outside, for me to climb out. And, oh yes, I was in a suit and heels.

Thankfully, after about half an hour, my boss missed me, came looking and found me stuck inside the dumpster. He had to lift me out of it, or... All the one piece swim suits that I cut out of scrap paper and taped onto the Pin-Up photos on the walls and the slid-out trays in the desks of all the guys, or...

From DICK DUNLAP, Launch Pad Construction

Trouble and Turnaround at LC-36, the Cape

(Plus a Tale of a Cute Blonde)

After graduating from Penn State in 1962, I went to work for GD Astronautics in San Diego. In late 1963, I married Nona, a very cute blond I had met in San Diego and who loved to play the "dumb blond" role. Shortly after our marriage, we transferred to Cape Canaveral where I worked on constructing Launch Complex 36B, which I had helped design while I was in San Diego. The Centaur project was falling behind schedule, and the program was in danger of being canceled. The first Atlas-Centaur launch exploded in mid-flight, and AC-3 and AC-4 were not totally successful.

By late 1964, NASA decided to stop the construction of 36B. However, on March 2, 1965, AC-5 was launched from 36A, and it exploded on the pad. Suddenly we were frantic to complete 36B. We were able to finish it, and we launched AC-6 from 36B on August 11, 1965. The mission was a complete success, and it likely saved the entire Centaur program from cancellation.

Everyone was so relieved and happy, the company threw a very big launch party at one of the motels in Cocoa Beach. Everyone was there, including Grant Hansen, the vice-president in charge of the entire Centaur program, and Dan Sarokon, the Test Conductor for both 36A and 36B. Our wives were invited to the party, and it was a very elaborate affair.

I wanted to introduce my cute young blond wife to Grant and Dan, so we went over to where the two of them were standing together. I said, "Nona, this is Grant Hansen, our Vice-President from San Diego in charge of the entire Centaur program, and this is Dan Sarokon, our Test Conductor. He is the one who pushes the button to launch." My wife batted her eyes, looked at me with all seriousness, and said, in her best dumb blond voice, "But Honey, you told me you were the Test Conductor."

I was quite taken aback, to say the least, and both Grant and Dan were doubled over with laughter. I'm sure the look on my face was priceless. Everyone seemed to get a big kick out of it except me. Anyway, that was the best Launch Party I ever attended, and my wife made it very memorable. She has pulled other tricks on me over the years, but that was one of her best. We are still married, and she has made my life very interesting.

From KEN KREBS

Getting good data can sometimes not be easy

GD and NASA Lewis Research Center (Lerc) decided to send personnel to the Tracking Station in South Africa to obtain near real-time results of the first second burn attempt after a coast phase. Several GD managers considered taking this prized trip, but wisely decided to use flight data analysis personnel for the task.

I was chosen to cover the Avionics Systems and Ernie Gravelle was chosen to cover the Mechanical Systems. Upon arrival in Pretoria, South Africa, after thirty-five hours of travel, we rented a British

Morris Minor car (mini four-seater, steering wheel on right, manual shift on left). Ernie did not want to drive, so I was elected.

Being exhausted from travel, my focus was not the best. Driving on the left side of the road, we had to make a right turn toward the hotel. Well my natural habits led me to turn into the right lane. Big mistake! I heard a loud horn and saw a large garbage truck coming straight at me. I dodged into a driveway on the right, avoiding the imminent collision. Not a good start.

Our task was to analyze Telemetry strip charts that we had previously set up with the tracking station. In those days the only communication was Telegraph Wire, expensive landline telephone (cable on the bottom of the ocean) and a radio link. The only surface large enough to roll out the strip charts was an empty trailer located about a half a block from the communication center where we rolled the strip charts out on the floor.

Well, after several launch delays, AC-4 was finally launched on December 11, 1964. Acquisition of the Centaur stage Telemetry signal occurred as planned. After the pass, the real-time strip charts were given to us to take to the trailer. GD management had set up a telephone link from SD and NASA Lerc set up the radio link from Cleveland.

It was quickly obvious that the main engines did not start and that the Centaur Vehicle was tumbling. Of course, our managers at GD and Cleveland wanted all the answers yesterday, not giving us time to analyze the data. How could we communicate results with them over two links, when the data was a half a block away? Ernie and I switched between communications and data analysis as best we could, running back and forth, to answer their questions.

Management finally decided to give us time to do our thing and would call back later. We quickly discovered that the settling engines were not keeping the propellants aft in the propellant tanks and that LH_2 was venting through the forward vent valve. That caused the vehicle to tumble, throwing the LH_2 forward and starving the boost pumps of propellant.

No time for sightseeing, we had to take the first available flight home (another thirty-five hours travel time) with the Telemetry tapes. I was fortunate (or unfortunate) to make two more trips to SA for the AC-8 and AC-9 two-burn test flights. AC-9 was the first success.

From DONNA GIBSON SHUFFLER

"OUCH, THAT SMARTS (AND NOT VERY SMART!)"

During my 39 years at GD I had many funny times. One of these that stands out most was the time I was sitting at my desk and Ray Niski came to tell me something. I started laughing. When I did I leaned forward and inadvertently dropped my breasts into my partially opened desk drawer. At the same time, while leaning forward and laughing, I closed the drawer on them.

Needless to say it was VERY painful. I turned blue and Ray left the office.

From TOM PHILLIPP, at the Cape

SOMEBODY HAS A PROBLEM?

Another "fond memory" is from the Gemini Program, wherein the Atlas launched an Agena upper stage into orbit, and the Titan on an adjacent launch site boosted the Gemini manned capsule with two astronauts aboard into the same orbit ninety minutes later, after Agena's first orbit, to rendezvous and dock with it. (Atlas and Titan had a very competitive history as they were developed concurrently as ICBM's for lucrative production contracts.) Rendezvous and docking was an essential process that had to be mastered for use on the Apollo Program to the moon.

At T-15 minutes during Flight Control Final System Checks, we had an indication on the recorder that an Atlas gyro went bad—but it could've been the amplifier in the ground support equipment inside the launcher test stand. The first thing we do is advise the Launch Director that we have a problem, then pursue a verification and resolution of it.

Minutes later, on the communication net: "Flight Control, what is your status? Are you 'Go' or 'No Go' for launch?" Before I could respond, another voice came over the net: **"Atlas Launch Director, this is NASA Mission Control, Houston. Terminate your launch operations for the day; <u>Titan</u> has a problem."**

FROM MAGGIE LIMA

MORE PERSONAL HUMOROUS TIMES WITH GD AT THE CAPE FROM DAYS LONG PAST

…All the one-piece swim suits that I cut out of scrap paper and taped onto the Pin-Up photos on the walls and the slide-out trays in the desks of all the guys, or

…The time the Department Chief chained the bumper of a car to a post in the ground outside Hangar K because one of the Material guys was famous for leaving for Patrick AFB to check on our parts order status on Fridays at noon, and never returning, or

…The time the draftsmen put lead shavings from an automatic pencil sharpener onto the head band inside a hard hat of one of the engineers who shaved his head. Nice black circle around the top of his head, which he couldn't see, for the rest of the day, or

…The time I signed up to take a CPR class, and was told, MEN ONLY, sorry.

FROM JERRY HUSTON

MALE-FEMALE COLLEAGUE RELATIONSHIP SAGA— ARE YOU READY FOR THIS ONE???

One day, while sitting at my desk in building fifty-one along Pacific Highway, I looked up and saw a herd of new employees being escorted to their departments by a member of the Personnel Department (That was before we had Human Resources). Being single, I always gave the new girls a once over. I must have said something about one particular girl to an associate of mine, Fred Winston, who was standing nearby.

A day or so after that event, the girl I had paid particular attention to came up to me and said, "Did y'all call me flamingo legs?" Not being associated with southern lexicon, I turned around to see who she was talking to when she said "y'all." There wasn't anyone there but me. I did the best to assure her that I didn't say such a thing and that I wasn't that kind of guy. She said, "Well, that other guy over there came over and said you did." With that, she stomped off and headed back to the Standards Group.

I liked her spunk, as well as her looks, so, one day, I bit the bullet and called her on the phone. We chatted for a while, then I asked her for a date. Then, she wanted to know my name, so I told her "Jerry Huston." Her answer to my request was a quick "No," then she hung up. My pride was absolutely destroyed.

 Since it is not my nature to accept "No" for answer, I called her back in a couple days. I said, "Do you still believe I called you flamingo legs? How could you have something against me when you don't even know me?" Her answer startled me. "Because you're married," she said. I thought that some of the girls I had dated only one time were getting even with me and spreading lies. Come to find out there was a fat little guy in the area who had been flirting with her, and she thought I was him. We shared the same last name.

Once we got that settled, she agreed to go out with me. I have been married to "flamingo legs" for fifty-four years now.

From TOM CHITTY, Assistant Test Conductor on LC-12 and LC-36 (received from Leroy Gross)

Smoke around an Atlas maybe not so good

After an explosion on the pad (likely AC-5), all of the wiring from blockhouse to pad had to be spliced in to the transfer room. When this BIG job was complete, Murphy Wardman was given the honor of throwing the "ON" switch to apply power to the system for the first, time. Unbeknown to Murph, one of our techs had run a plastic tube, from the Power panel to a slightly remote location.

When Murph threw the switch to 'ON" applying power to the system for the first time after the reconstruction the tech took a long drag on his cigarette and blew into the tube. When Murph saw the smoke rising from the panel he turned white. Later he laughed.

From TOM LEECH, Guidance Analysis

Outdoors calling, let's explore, and we did

Having arrived from the state of Indiana in 1959 to join the Astronautics Division, I had little experience dealing with the outdoors world of San Diego and Southern California. "What's a desert? Baja, where's that?"

Fortunately the GD Adventurers Club provided a way to find out about nature here. With them, and knowledgeable leaders, we went on hikes, backpacks, overnight camping in the desert, even journeys down to Baja's wild scene. On many of those, children were included so this gave me a way to engage my daughter, usually with a pal or two, into outdoors adventuring.

One trip in the late sixties was a bit further away. With a four-day weekend off work, the Adventurers headed over into Arizona to Havasu Canyon, a side territory from the Grand Canyon. We headed over right after work on Wednesday, arriving well into the night, and camped in cars, maybe campers, and the ground. On Thanksgiving Day, we loaded up our backpacks and headed down into barren country toward where the Havasupai tribe had their modest village and from there we would head further down into the canyon.

Since we had various levels of backpacking capability, we were a bit strung out during that trek in. After a few hours we arrived at the start of a river, which appeared right out of the ground. It kept growing, with a lovely turquoise color and eventually would create a full-blown river with three fine waterfalls. This would be in the area where we camped.

I and a few others finally made it to the small village, with maybe a small market, a small church and a group of houses. We paused briefly, then continued on to meet the whole group for our Friday and Saturday explorations. That was when we heard a story that made a few of us mutter a few laments that we had missed the boat.

And what was that? Well, the front walkers had arrived an hour or so before us stragglers. As they walked past that small church, they noticed many of the locals were seated around tables and about to partake of a delightful Thanksgiving dinner. To which they invited those several Adventurers to join them, and of course, possibly to not offend the locals Hah!—they did. So while the rest of us were still diligently making our way inward, they enjoyed a sit-down dinner with turkey, mashed potatoes, cranberry pudding, and apple pie.

Then they headed onward to make the camping area ready for the group. We wandered in, a few at a time, and pulled our Thanksgiving dinners from our backpacks, mostly dehydrated chicken stews and GORP (Good Old Raisins and Peanuts), consumed while the early arrivals watched and I'm sure chuckled with amusement. Is there a moral here? (We all managed to have a most enjoyable visit in the magnificent Havasu Canyon, though every Thanksgiving I recall how those selected few had their own special dinner, the dirty scoundrels.)

From JOHN MEDINA, Security

ONE SMALL WHAA FOR MANKIND???

GD was testing a vehicle for Hughes Aircraft Company at a building at the far end of the Kearny Mesa property, close to the Maxwell Labs Building. All personnel were required to wear lab coats, caps, booties and white gloves. The article being tested was called 'The Moon Lander' which was designed to take moon soil samples and send results back.

One evening all personnel left for their evening meal. I was the lone security person there. The structure housing the item was enclosed in a very large teepee-like tent. I said to myself, "If that is going to the moon, I have to take a look at it." I unzipped the opening and walked around it marveling at this structure. It was a giant tripod in configuration, with a small under-belly housing. Below that was a small scooper-like device. The legs of this giant tripod and vehicle were covered with gold foil.

After one more walk-around, I stopped and said to myself, "If this thing is going to the moon, my thumb print is going to the moon." I took off my right-hand white glove and gently pressed my right thumb against the gold leaf tripod leg.

The vehicle was successfully launched and sent data back to earth. And one small thumb print landed on the moon. I've told no one about this before. But now, when I look up at the moon, I remember Neil Armstrong and the rest of the astronauts, and one small thumb print that hitched a ride on a gold leaf tripod leg. "Look up Tom! Full moon!" (marking the day of the August blue moon, appearing shortly after Neil Armstrong's passing).

San Diego AIAA Chapter won big national honor, with all GD guys on the local board. Bill Chana (Chair), Tom Leech, John Wild, Fred Porter, Jim Mason. Photo use approved by San Diego AIAA Chapter

FROM ED HUJSAK

FLUORINE HELPS ROCKETS, MAYBE

Outside of the rocket community the word flox might get one thinking about decorating Christmas trees, or perhaps something to do with keeping the dentist happy. But for genuine rocket people the term applies to a mixture of the elements fluorine and oxygen to serve as the oxidizer in rocket engines. A rocket engine that consumes fluorine will yield higher performance than one that consumes oxygen. But fluorine is nasty stuff to handle, deadly poisonous, and unless one is very careful, prone to set fire to whatever it is exposed to.

More easily handled, but still treacherous is a mixture of fluorine and oxygen (FLOX), in their liquid states, with the concentration of fluorine at about ten percent. This mixture was of interest for Atlas because the payload weight was predicted to rise by about ten per cent.

During the mid-sixties Bill Roberts from the Program Office rounded up some development money and Alan Schuler, from my pre-design group, one of the finest engineers I ever worked with, got assigned to run tests in which the propellant mixture would flow through propellant lines at the Sycamore Canyon missile test site. In the course of time the equipment came smoothly together and an arrangement of pipes, valves and tanks was assembled for the test. A load of FLOX was delivered and loaded into the test fixture. Came the day for the flow test, with the experiment fully instrumented, the test crew and observers, including Alan and Bill, sealed themselves in the blockhouse and proceeded with operations that led to finally beginning the propellant flow.

Through the blockhouse window there was initially no sign of anything occurring. But then in rapid succession there was a puff of smoke, then what looked like a fire, then a conflagration that looked like it was going to consume the entire tower.

When things died down and everything was under control the unflappable Alan Schuler stood at a blockhouse window, eyeing the wreckage, mindful of a plume of poisonous fluorine gas that was drifting down the canyon toward Santee.

"Well," he said, "That didn't work."

FROM JOHN MEDINA, SECURITY GUARD

"FLOX, PHLOK, FLOCKS OF PHEASANTS AT SYCAMORE CANYON TEST SITE."

The perimeter chain link fence surrounding the site had not been completed, however a temporary three strands of barbed wire fence was surrounding the site. At one point we heard gunshot fire coming from the Sycamore Canyon toward Santee, about a half mile from site one.

We went to investigate. There were several hunters in all their garb, several pick-up trucks and wire cages. Some hunters had crossed through and over the barbed wire fence, chasing pheasants with their guns.

We stopped them and informed them that they were trespassing on Air Force property (government property) and that they would have to leave the area on this side of the fence.

They were very friendly and agreed to cooperate. We chatted awhile. They explained they were member of the "Santee Co-op Shoot Club", that the pheasants were grain-fed in pens. When they were nice and plump they would be released and the birds would fly off. In this case, most of them flew onto the government property.

They released a lot of pheasants, so much so, that for quite some time the pheasants would just be strutting along the site roads and fire breaks. Three of us decided this would be good eating! We made some slingshots and got ball bearings from the tool crib; we didn't miss! And they were delicious! Reminded me of Colorado pheasants where I grew up. There you would just drive down a country road, one would usually fly into the radiator of your car, and there was your dinner!

ED "SPIKE" WOLFENSBERGER

MORE SYCAMORE—PLEASE TELL THEM TO STOP MAKING DOORS!

At the Sycamore Canyon test sites, the blockhouses and the transfer rooms had rows and rows of equipment cabinet racks containing recorders and signal conditioning equipment. When Centaur started, new requirements drove the need for a new test stand at Sycamore site S2, requiring some more racks.

The designs for electronic racks for Atlas testing was originally contracted to a firm named Radiophone that no longer existed when this new need arose. A full set of the Radiophone drawings could be found in the blue print crib and we would use those to either modify or repair existing equipment. I believe that it was John Duddy who had the assignment to build and install signal-conditioning equipment in the new Centaur test stand transfer room.

The basic structure of each of those racks was fairly simple, consisting largely of Uni-strut^{TM} channel and sheet aluminum. Access to each cabinet's wiring was through a hinged, latching rear door whose main functions were to contain the cooling air from a blower at the bottom. The door also required an inside box-like pocket containing the wiring tabulation listing for each cabinet.

Though the rest of the cabinets and their contents were progressing OK, for some reason the shop had difficulty manufacturing the four or five tear doors that John needed to complete the task. After much negotiation with Shop Planning, the doors began to take shape.

One morning as we were arriving for work John was on the phone with the shop and he could be heard exasperatedly saying "Well, tell them to stop making doors, I only need five! Why can't you tell them to stop making doors! But I don't need any more doors." To the rest of us it sounded as if they had a production line going and didn't want to stop! He said, "I'll be right out," as he hung up the phone and headed out the door for the shop. He left us with a vision of something like Disney's "Sorcerer's Apprentice" trying to stop the water buckets!

Was this the end of the story? Not Likely! The cabinets with their installed equipment were finally finished. Now they had to be sent out to Sycamore. As they were being fork lifted onto a truck, and not being secured, some of them fell from the forklift and landed on the pavement with considerable damage. I think John thought his efforts were cursed though they did have some extra doors to use in rebuilding the ill-fated racks. It was about a year later that John Duddy resigned and went back to school at the University of San Diego to study Law.

From BILL KETCHUM

What was appropriate test conductor wardrobe?

When we were testing new rocket propellants at Convair Sycamore Canyon Site "D" in the late 1960s, on one occasion we were preparing for a test and a dozen of us engineers and technicians were gathered together in the blockhouse waiting for the test conductor, Hal Brittain, to arrive.

Finally he showed up, covered in blood and smelling awful. He told us that on his way up the winding road he had hit and killed a deer. Rather than leave it there he and his passenger skinned and gutted the deer and threw it in the back of his pickup truck.

After explaining all this we proceeded with the test. For those who never met Hal he was a big man, probably weighing close to 300 pounds. I still have a vivid recollection of him standing there in his bloody coveralls.

From TOM LEECH, Guidance Analysis, Kearny Mesa

Murphy keeps showing up

My manager, a couple levels up, Frank Anthony, was a good presenter and diligent in making sure he had the right gear for his presentations. For this one he would use flip charts and had definitely requested a chart holder. Well done—ready to go. Except, later he moaned that when he got to the room, he had a chart holder all right, except it was one you placed posters onto a ledge, and his charts needed one they could hang from. Made for a frustrating use of charts. Murphy won again.

Frank and I were over at NASA Langley in Virginia for a meeting. It went on awhile, no surprise, and we finally headed out of the facility. As we walked fast to our rental car, Frank asked me "What time is it?" I replied I didn't know as I never carried a watch. Frank was a free-spirited beach fan, surfer and volley-baller on weekends and said, **"Guys like us should not be allowed to travel together. I never wear a watch either."**

CHAPTER 5—1970s

Primary operations at General Dynamics (GD): Convair San Diego, Cape Canaveral, Florida and Vandenberg AFB.

Programs included:

- Atlas space booster
- Centaur upper stage rocket
- Tomahawk Cruise Missiles
- DC-10 Fuselage

In the early phase of the Convair Cruise Missile (CM) program organization was a major and arduous proposal effort between GD CM and the buyer, the United States Navy. A series of humorous cartoons was created by artist Tommy Thompson from Art and Editorial, triggered by GD Proposal Manager Ed Velton and with the friendly eyes of Convair CM leadership. These got lots of laughs from the players involved and others in the GD San Diego world. Key players in the early program, and cartoons, were Captain Locke, U.S. Navy and Ralph Mackenzie, Convair CM leader. Here are a few of those cartoons. (We wanted to get an OK from Tommy T but he has passed on as far as we know.)

"GENTLEMEN, ONLY A FEW MORE HOURS OF AGONIZING AND WE WILL HAVE THE PROPOSAL COLOR SELECTED."

"DID THEY HURT US MUCH?" (REFERENCE TO PROPOSAL REVIEWERS, THE RED TEAM)

FUN ON THE JOB

"RELAX CAPTAIN, WE'RE PUTTING THE PROPOSAL ON THE AIRPLANE RIGHT NOW!"

WOW! THAT PROPOSAL JOB IS DONE! HELLO FAMILIES.

FROM BARBARA L. SMITH, KEARNY MESA

WATCH THOSE SECRET DOCUMENTS

I used to work for Bob Lynch on the cruise missile, my name is Barbara Smith (one of the six Barbara Smith's that worked there).

Bob was leaving on a trip to Washington and asked me to get a secret package ready for him to carry on the plane. I finally got him out the door to catch his flight. A short time later I got a call from him; he was at the airport and wanted to know if he left his secret package on his desk. Of course not I said, I distinctly know that I gave you the package. We worked in Building One on the sixth floor on Kearny Mesa and I watched him get into his car; he laid the secret package on the roof while loading his bags in the trunk. At that moment my phone rang and I left the window to answer it. When I returned to the window the car was gone out of site.

 Several days went by and some man came into the lobby with a bunch of eight by ten sheets of paper that looked like they had been run over several times. He said that he used to work at GD and was driving down Route 15 and noticed the papers scattered about. His curiosity got the best of him, so he got out of the car every several yards and picked up these papers. Of course he knew immediately that they were classified and that someone must have dropped them from their car. The girl in the lobby called me because she saw Bob's name on some of the pages. Of course, it wasn't funny then, but I get a chuckle out it now. They sent some of the guards out to clean up the freeway and capture as much as they could. No, Bob didn't get fired!

FUN ON THE JOB

FROM JERRY BUTSKO

MORE ABOUT THAT PREVIOUS TALE FROM BARBARA SMITH ABOUT BOB LYNCH

The rest of the story is: I was with Bob on that trip and rode with him from Kearny Mesa to the airport. He discovered the loss of the double wrapped package when we got to the airport parking lot and called his office (I guess it was Barb who took his call and started the search from that end!) We headed to Washington, DC on an American Airlines flight.

Somehow GD security started communicating with Bob via the co-pilot, who kept coming back to Bob with questions. I seem to recall that Bob found out while we were in DC that the package was found. I also recall that the package, which Bob determined he had put on the roof of his car while he put his luggage in the car, slid off the car as we drove down Old Route 395 to Mission Valley. When found, the package was torn open and the poor soul who rescued it but didn't return it to Kearny Mesa for a while was interrogated by GD Security who wondered what he had done with it!

So much for being a good citizen!

FROM SPIKE WOLFENSBERGER

FLORIDA HAS LOTS OF WATER, BUT WHERE IS IT ESPECIALLY WHEN YOU REALLY NEED IT?

In Florida, an office trailer became our office at Kennedy Space Center for overseeing the installation of that huge TV system at Launch Complex 39, the origin of the Apollo Moon launches. The trailer was located just south of the vehicle assembly building within a short walking distance to the LC-39 Launch Center.

In addition to our engineering needs, it also had a bathroom, but that required water at least to flush the toilet. Vern Boyer, our on-site program manager contacted the Army Corps of Engineers representative who said we had to have a well.

"OK, where?"

"Right alongside the trailer," was the response.

The well driller came to the trailer and proceeded to sink a hole. I think we hit water at about ten feet, but it was black as coal with an overpowering sulfurous smell. They kept drilling and at about twice as deep we found clear artesian water. It was under pressure so we needed no pump. It was, however so mineralized that it had to be filtered and then put through a water softener before it was even suitable to use for just flushing a toilet.

Yes, we had to have a septic tank too. I remember every Friday Vern Boyer would attack the toilet to keep it operating and free of mineralization.

From BILL VEGA

POWER OF A GOOD VISUAL AID (REMEMBER THE OVERHEAD PROJECTOR?)

There are all sorts of anecdotes involving the ACM (Advance Cruise Missile) program. Here is one of the best:

As you may remember there were three competitors for the next generation Air Force air launched cruise missile:

- Boeing, who was the contractor for the current program,
- Lockheed Skunk Works who had been on contract behind the door for some time to the tune of nearly a billion dollars
- and GD the contractor for the Navy cruise missile.

Boeing was, of course, the Air Force favorite. What Air Force General would want to do business with a Navy contractor? As the competition heightened, Boeing made a strong pitch saying that why would the government want to have a competitor develop a brand new missile while all the ALCM would need to do was to fly inverted, and in this way the inlet would be masked leading to a vehicle with a low RADAR signature. A simple development process at best. Of course, this simplistic pitch was far from the real story.

When we perceived that the Air Force was giving this approach serious consideration, we swung into action. I set up a small team comprised of all the key disciplines and tasked them to act as a Boeing team and develop the work statement covering the necessary studies, designs and tests in order to accomplish the inverted ALCM approach.

Ten days later, work statement in hand, we hit the Pentagon. The Boeing discussion had clearly been superficial and, even if the very significant development was entered into, it wasn't clear that the inverted ALCM would have a low signature or the necessary range for safe standoff. We accompanied our presentation with a viewgraph that said it all. We found out later that the viewgraph was making the rounds of the Pentagon Air Force generals' offices accompanied by peals of laughter echoing down the halls. Needless to say the Inverted ALCM died a sudden death. (Below is the GD view graph that said it all, and maybe won the contract.)

SUPERFICIAL CHANGES DO NOT
CREATE STEALTH SYSTEMS

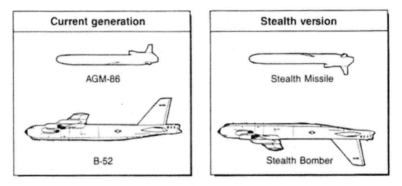

Current generation	Stealth version
AGM-86	Stealth Missile
B-52	Stealth Bomber

Bottom Line

If the AGM-86B configuration is so amenable to signature reduction, why has it been so difficult to attain the current ALCM goals?

FROM HAL SIMONS

MURPHY'S LAW AT WORK

After reading the interesting stories in your last email I felt I could add one of my own. This is the gist of the Final Test Report on the Tomahawk Recovery System

I was responsible for running some interesting Tomahawk tests. Engineers at a test facility on San Clemente Island, 68 miles west of San Diego, were launching Tomahawks westward over the ocean to assess operation of its avionics. At flight termination the Tomahawk would drop into the ocean and sink. To prevent this very expensive loss, a flotation bag system was designed to buoy the Tomahawk until it could be recovered. A water sensor was located in the underside of the Tomahawk to trigger ejection of the bag cover plate and release the orange bag as it inflates from a high pressure air canister. Static tests had indicated that the bag's size was sufficient to float the Tomahawk.

The tests proceeded at San Clemente, but on splashdown the Tomahawk sank with no flotation bag in sight. The design engineers proposed some possible causes:

1. The water sensor did not produce the trigger to start bag deployment.
2. The bag was packed in a manner preventing its deployment.
3. The air canister failed to sufficiently inflate the bag.
4. The cover plate did not eject when commanded and prevented the bag deployment.
5. Sharp edges left by the cover plate damaged the bag causing it to leak.

POSSIBILITY TESTS

At Kearny Mesa, I was given the task to investigate these possibilities and report. A test panel was fabricated with a production bag, its cavity, a cover plate and compressed air canister:

1. Several sensors were immersed in water with each generating the correct trigger.

2. Regardless of the method of packing, with the cover plate removed, the bag fully inflated and

3. Maintained its pressure over a period of over two hours.

4/5. This possibility test was a little more complicated. Near the Environmental Lab our test panel with the bag and canister was bolted to a heavy platform and the bag's cover plate was installed. A line was connected to carry a simulated sensor signal to start the deployment sequence.

It was expected that the ejected cover would fly some distance and possibly cause damage in the adjacent employee parking lot. To prevent damage a heavy rope mesh tent was hoisted over the platform to catch the cover plate. The Design Engineers and my Lead Engineer were called to review the test setup. They agreed that the setup should provide the desired results and authorized the test.

With video cameras on, instrumentation and audio recorders recording, and with numerous observers, the countdown was started at five. At zero the initiation signal was given, the cover plate ejected up into the mesh and the bag deployed fully inflated. Then, the unexpected happened! Rebounding from the overhead mesh the cover plate struck the inflated bag causing a gash which deflated the bag. Murphy's Law! On review of the recordings and the flotation bag system components it was determined that the test had shown that the system operated satisfactorily and that it was highly unlikely that the cover plate would cause similar damage to the bag when deployed over water. As a result, the cause of the flotation bag system failures had not been determined and further testing was needed.

SPLASHDOWN TEST

A new test was devised to drop a Tomahawk with a complete recovery system minus the cover plate into Convair's large pool with video and still cameras filming the event. A net was strung across the pool at a depth of ten feet to hold the Tomahawk if the flotation failed. Fifteen feet above the pool, a sling holding the Tomahawk horizontally was suspended by a tall crane in a sling which had a remotely activated release mechanism. Cameras were arranged around the pool as well as at the underwater viewing ports. All recorders and cameras were to start recording at T-minus-10 seconds. I was to use a bullhorn for the countdown and trigger the release mechanism at T-0.

A large crowd had gathered to watch the show. I started the countdown at T-10 and at T-0 I triggered the release. When the Tomahawk hit the water the bag deployed fully inflated but the Tomahawk's weight and momentum carried it well under water. That force was enough to rip the bag from the Tomahawk allowing it to sink to the net below.

This test result showed that the flotation bag was not strong enough to hold the Tomahawk. It was decided rather than redesign the system for water recovery, future test flights would be to desert targets with parachute recovery.

FROM LELAND E. (LEE) BOLT

REVEALING INTENSE HIRING PROCESS

In the rapid build-up of the Tomahawk program, we were hiring Logistics and Support System Integration personnel. Remembering the early experience, we looked in the Human Resources Department Miscellaneous folder. We hired two people, because Tomahawk needed them. Each did good jobs in our department for about a year, then went to other departments.

One became Tomahawk Marketing Director and the other transferred to Guidance Analysis. Her resume indicated she had a Bachelor of Arts and Master's in Music, and most of her Ph.D. in Music Theory. Her references included Dr. Fawcett and Ben Carrol of Fort Worth Division. Both said hire her, even before they knew the job description. They said she had great special relations concepts and could solve the Rubik's Cube in record time. Looking in the Miscellaneous File paid off.

From BETTY MCLAUGHLIN, Advanced Technology Group

Slip sliding away...

Do you remember when facilities closed every other bathroom in Building Four (Kearny Mesa) just to save money? I believe that was the first early attempt at downsizing the hourly janitors. Well, I was walking up the hallway headed towards Building Three when a high ranking Air Force officer stopped to ask me where the closest men's room was because the one he wanted to use had a padlock on it.

I pointed down the hall but suggested he not use that one because it was overflowing due to heavy usage so he would need to continue further. Of course he was perplexed but I explained that facilities management was saving "resources" and he made a comment about why Convair needed to save money on toilet paper.

He marched ahead of me and promptly slipped and fell on his butt from the bathroom overflow—it was a hard fall and his uniform was a mess. It was quite a sight and gave those who witnessed the fall quite a giggle. A few days later, all bathroom padlocks had been removed and there was no doubt in my mind as to why.

FUN ON THE JOB

FROM HOWARD BONESTEEL

SOMETIMES TOUGH TO CLEAR FOR LAUNCH

From Atlas Recollections—Atlas 50th book 1957-2007

Getting ready to launch Atlas Centaur-45, High Energy Astronomy Observatory (HEAO) A, the weather was terrible with heavy rain and lots of lightning. We held the count for a long time, finally got clearance, then held for a shrimp boat escaping the storm. We tried to radio them to clear the impact area, no luck. Sent helicopter out to clear the area. Finally got through on the radio and the reply was, "Talk louder, can't hear you, there's a god-damn helicopter here, lots of noise!"

FROM: CLAY PERKINS, Centaur Engineering

WATCH FOR THOSE COMMIES ON THE JOB

One day in the mid-sixties I wore my "F_ _ _ COMMUNISM" pin to work on the second floor of Building Twenty-six (Kearny Mesa facility). Got a lot of laughs. My boss (Rich Wilson or Dan Heald, I don't remember) ignored it, but the parallel supervisor, Del Casale, came over and told me to take it off. Language back then had not coarsened like today. The engineering areas back then were a vast plain of desks interspaced by rectilinear walkways. Well, I stood up and asked Del, "Are you a Communist?"

That made him mad and again told me to take it off, getting pretty loud. By then there must have been a hundred engineers looking at us. I said, "No, it's my First Amendment right to wear it!" Del turned around and started to walk away, yelling over his shoulder, "You take it **off** or you will be fired!"

As he walked down the aisle, I pointed at his retreating back and shouted, "That man is a Communist!" Now the whole floor was watching and laughing. I wore the badge for the rest of the day and never heard anything further from Del or anyone else.

From WARREN REAVIS, Atlas-Centaur Business Development

EGG ON YOUR COLLEAGUES

Hello Tom, given your invitation to document amusing events in those special days, here is a true event that occurred at General Dynamics during my time there. This favorite story occurred with John D. Engunier (** real name not used to protect reputation, and keep off future grave marker).

There was one morning when I was carefully pouring my home made coffee from the thermos and took great pains to avoid the grounds of coffee still floating at the top of my noxious brew. At that moment, John D. had stopped at my desk to watch my delicate process. When he asked what that stuff was, I replied it is my concept of Ahobo coffee. I explained that this particular morning my coffee maker had given up its ghost and I was on my own. In response, he suggested that there was a way to get the coffee grounds to settle by cracking an egg in the mixture. I thanked him for his sage advice and promised to try the egg solution.

On that following morning, my coffee ritual was modified as I carefully avoided a rather sickly green egg floating at the top of my thermos brew. The egg yolk had apparently turned from its normal yellow color to what I would call "Goose Turd Green" and the egg white 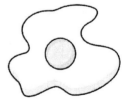 now looked like a thick layer of phlegm as it bobbed up and down in my experimental coffee.

At that moment, John D. stopped by and asked how the coffee was this morning. I responded "I've had better coffee but this will do for now" and then offered to allow him to try some. When John D.

poured the coffee he apparently did not hear the plop as the night-mare fell into his cup. As our conversation continued, John D. was looking at me as he took his first sip and then felt something brush against his lips.

At that moment all conversation stopped as he slowly looked down at his cup. As I recall, everything seemed to be in slow motion as his eyes extended from their normal position, looking very much like a Road Runner cartoon character, as he stared in horror at that alien floating object in his cup. It was only by quick reaction that I was able to dodge the spew of coffee coming from his mouth as he yelled out "What is that?" Actually I think he said something more descriptive; however, I would like to keep this story pure for more innocent people than me.

I explained to John D. that this was the egg that was supposed to settle the coffee grounds. After composing himself as best he could, he explained that the egg was not to be left in the coffee but only to settle the grounds. For some reason that I can't explain John D. did not want to sample my coffee ever again.

My meeting with Admiral Hostettler (mid '70s)

Although the Ground launch Cruise Missile Program was an Air Force Project it was directed by the Joint Cruise Missile Office under the command of Admiral Hostettler. The flight tests were launched at the Dugway Proving Ground, directly south of The Great Salt Lake, Utah, and the flights were conducted over the Utah Test and Training Range. The Control Center was at Hill AFB near Ogden, Utah.

During launch and flight tests, I served as Chief Chartwatcher with a crew of engineers from GD, two Air Force Officers and a Civil Service Engineer from Hill. The test vehicles were equipped with recovery systems and our job was to monitor flight data displayed on strip charts and report any discrepancies to the test conductor so he could order "Terminate" or "Recovery" to save the vehicle. It was a rather cumbersome, time-consuming procedure as the information would have to travel from the chart watcher to me, from me to the GD Test Conductor, then to the Air Force Test Conductor, and finally relayed to the chase plane pilot who had the "Recovery Button."

On one such flight test we had a problem shortly after launch, during transition to cruise flight in which the missile crashed. The first I learned of the problem was when I heard over the radio net from the airborne test conductor who was seated in the back seat of the F-4 chase plane say "It's going in". As it turned out, there was telemetry data indicating a problem but it was very subtle and the young Air Force Lieutenant monitoring that data missed it. It was highly doubtful that we could have saved the missile anyway. After the flight, we learned from the data that we had apparently experienced a massive leak in the pneumatic system used to deploy the fins, deploy the engine air scoop, open the wing doors and deploy the wings, so that none of these events occurred.

Later, Air Force Lt. Colonel Otterson and I had a series of meetings to see if we could somehow come up with a plan that could lessen the extent of the damage in the event of a similar catastrophe. We decided that there were six measurements that would confirm successful transition to cruise flight and arranged them all on one chart so that I could observe them myself and wouldn't have to rely on the individual Chartwatchers. I would be in direct contact with the airborne test conductor and could order "Terminate" during the launch/transition period. It was generally understood that at its heaviest weight with a full load of fuel and insufficient altitude to fully deploy the chutes it was unlikely to safely recover the missile. But we hoped at least to slow the descent and get back bigger pieces of hardware to determine the cause of the failure.

We had a meeting at GD to explain the plan to Admiral Hostettler. The first thing he said when he sat down at the meeting table was **"The last thing I want is for some dumb shit to punch out a good bird!"**

During the presentation by Lt. Col. Otterson, my name was mentioned a number of times. When the presentation was over, GD's Vice-president in charge of the Ground Launch Cruise Missile Program, Bernie Kuchta, said to the Admiral, "By the way, that's Art Imdieke seated behind you."

We both stood. He turned around and I said " Good morning Admiral. I'm the dumb shit who will try not to punch out a good bird."

He just smiled and said "Do good work."

P.S. I monitored the remainder of our test launches with heart in throat but never had to issue a "Terminate" command as all subsequent test launches were successful.

From Ted Lamoureux

GD's key to getting along with the Russkies

From his My life at Convair.

Around 1975 I became the Engineering Chief of Failure Analysis. Somewhat later we not only had the Atlas missile, the Centaur missile, and the Cruise missile, but we had also started investigative work on the Advanced Cruise Missile (ACM). The Cruise missile was of a size to be launched by a submarine while submerged. It was contained inside of a metal tube for ease in handling into the sub or into the launch tubes of a missile frigate. Actually Cruise missiles were launched from the battleship, USS *Wisconsin* (BB-64) during the first Iraqi war. We also developed the capability to launch the regular cruise missile from a trailer for mobility in Europe as a Ground Launched Cruise Missile (GLCM) with a nuclear warhead. This version was addressed during the Reagan Administration in what was known at the Strategic Arms Limitation Talks (SALT) between the United States and the Former Soviet Union.

As a result of the treaty, the Russians had the right to inspect our trailer manufacturing area whenever they wanted without prior notification. The U.S. also could inspect the Russian facilities that were part of the SALT treaty. The Russians started the visits, and after the tour, our management and Security Chief would take them to the upper management cafeteria for lunch. It was a fancy lunch room with tablecloths and cloth napkins. The cafeteria people made a chocolate chip cookie about five inches in diameter and one-third of an inch thick. Well, the Russians fell in love with the cookies and ate some, put some in their pockets, and told the rest of Russia about them. Soon we had more Russians than you could shake a stick at and all of them wanted lunch and cookies.

From Maggie Lima

More personal humorous times with GD at the Cape from days long past

Then there was the time Quality Assurance decided to play a prank while encapsulating a spacecraft at Astrotech, and in the nightly turn-over notes, fabricated a story about the fairings falling, destroying the spacecraft—yada-yada—not so funny! Or…

The time I was asked to type a letter for one of the guys in a different department to help out, but when he came back to get it, I hadn't had time to complete it yet and he told me that "I was flat" to which I simply crossed my arms in front of myself and told him that I couldn't help it, I was born that way, or…

The company picnics where I got to meet all the families of all the guys that I worked with every single day, lots of times hearing the wives tell the husbands as they walked away from meeting me, "That's Maggie, you told me she was old and fat." Now, that was pretty funny, considering that most of the guys were old enough to be my Dad!

From Tom Leech, Internal Communications/ Ombudsman, Kearny Mesa

You're talking about what?

In 1975, the Kearny Mesa operation assigned me to internal communications, including such duties as the weekly Blue Sheet, division ombudsman, and general team communication. I became part of the HR (Human Relations, or were they still calling it IR - Industrial Relations?) staff, with Bobby Foushee in charge. "Foush" and I were recent arrivals to HR, after previous lengthy duties in Business Development, Programs and Engineering.

I was giving an update about some current action over in the space booster game involving STS. About the third time I made that reference, I noted the company doctor was grinning. Oh, oh, my brain said, are we on the same wavelength? So I asked: "Doctor, why are you grinning?"

Replied the Doc: "What's STS?"

Oops, my goof, so I explained it as Space Transportation System, a very active project.

"Whew!" said the Doc," Thanks for clarifying that. In my medical profession, the term STS is well known. It refers to the Serological Test for Syphilis."

Lesson: got to watch those acronyms.

Those simplified terms can have staying power

I was teaching a course at Kearny Mesa about improving team presentations. One team came in with a fun presentation dealing with visits to that country below the border. An occasional problem comes up, so to speak, when we gringos eat too much of certain foods that later disagrees with us. Their topic was how to take care with what you ate and drank so that you would not have the BNB condition hit you when you were flying home. We listeners inquired as the what did that acronym mean? The answer—Bad News on the Baggage. Four decades later that term often appears when I'm on a plane.

COMMUNICATION COUNTS (AND IT CAN BE TRICKY)

The weekly company newsletter—the "Blue Sheet"—was in my bailiwick for a while. A high interest item was the number that appeared noting how many people were employed at Convair that week. Except one time it wasn't there. My phone started ringing early that Monday morning, and the rumors were sweeping the place. "Why wasn't the number there? Had a massive layoff occurred? Why was the company trying to hide it from us?" The truth was it just got left off. Productivity probably suffered badly for a few days because of that.

MORE FROM MURPHY

A colleague, "Roberto," was giving an important morning presentation to a high-level audience at the main conference room in Kearny Mesa Building Two. (the one with the spiral staircase). Right away he realized he did not have a pointer to focus audience attention to screen key points (this was with overhead projector). He gave me a quick "help?" look and I nodded and walked over to Building One, to the execs conference room on the second floor. I grabbed the pointer from there, walked quickly back to Building Two and gave my crony the pointer. "Hooray" he whispered and used it often during his presentation.

That afternoon he and I were at a meeting in that Building One conference room. Grant Hansen was the presenter and he reached to the usual spot to get the pointer, except no pointer. He was a bit miffed, and "Roberto" gulped an "OMG – I forget to put it back!" He darted out of the room, dashed back over to Building Two, got the pointer, brought it back and handed it to Grant. Lesson learned, the hard way.

WHERE THERE'S A WILL...

When Howard Hughes died, and wills started appearing from the woodwork as well as desert, we got a call from the Hughes people. Since GD had many dealings with him during the 880 jetliner years, was it possible that among all our files Howard's will could have been stashed? We looked but didn't locate one. Which doesn't mean it wasn't there, does it? Hmm, where are those file cabinets?

FROM MARY KLEMENT, CRUISE MISSILE (CM)

PRESENTATION TIME WITH A FEW TRAVEL WRINKLES THROWN IN

I was working on the Cruise Missile Program as the Manager of Logistics Engineering. Two colleagues (who shall remain nameless) and I had to make a presentation in Crystal City, Virginia, near the Pentagon, and travel booked us on flights together (or so I thought).

When we got to Dallas it turns out that my ticket took me through Chicago to DC while they had a direct flight! (What??? How did that happen). Anyway they left me and went to their gate and of course I got stuck in Chicago and didn't get into DC until eleven that evening.

When I arrived at the Marriott they had given away my room (it was cherry blossom time in the city). My two colleagues had arrived, didn't tell them I was still coming, and were fast asleep. I begged the Marriott to find something for me because I had the lead in the presentation the next morning and I needed some sleep. They called all over but no rooms were available anywhere.

They finally asked me if I was there for more than one night and I said "No" after my presentation we were getting back on a plane to San Diego.

So they put me in the Presidential Suite at the top of the hotel. It had a living room, dining room, fully stocked bar (which they told me was free) and a large bedroom with a steam shower. It also had newspapers from all over the world and what I came to find out later were a pair of cigar cutters on the living room table. I woke my colleagues up to gloat. Unfortunately they immediately headed to the penthouse and drank up all the liquor before I was able to throw them out. The next morning, at checkout, I had to face the management who said there was no charge but noted my remarkable capacity for alcohol.

From JACK SMOTHERS, Kearny Mesa Art and Editorial

Tuning up the Annual Report

GD Headquarters wanted a big color photo of smock-clad workers on the Tomahawk assembly line for the GD Annual Report. So they shot some stuff from off a ladder (maybe the lensman was Pete Autio). Anyway, when our betters saw the photos, they exclaimed, "My, god, we can't use these! The workers look like a bunch of druggies and drunks."

Never mind that these guys were the real deal.

"Reshoot the picture and get some people who look credible!" The deadline loomed, as they always did. So a Fleet-footed messenger (get it? Fleet?) raced from Building Five to Art and Editorial in nearby Building Two. They pulled a bunch of us off our regular jobs as artists, editors, con men, and hustled us to the assembly line.

George Paul and I happened to be in front for the new photo. We put on smocks and grabbed a wrench or whatever was handy. Someone told all of us fakes to make it look real, so George and I, one on each side of the Tomahawk, stuck our hands into the innards of the motor (the outside flap of the missile was up). I remember my tool (so to speak) hit a metal something in the engine. It wobbled. My only thought as they took the new picture was that, having no idea of what I was doing, I hadn't wrecked the damned thing. Evidently not.

FUN ON THE JOB

FROM RICK BRUSCH

HIRING ME OR FIRING ME?

From Atlas Recollections—Atlas 50th book 1957-2007

I worked on Launch Vehicle and interplanetary trajectory optimization. The day I started work, two aeronautical engineers were laid off. I thought I might be the last aerospace engineer to find employment after the Atlas Heyday. Job interview forms left over from the Atlas development program had four summary categories:

1) Must hire
2) Consider further for hire
3) Don't Hire
4) Hire if large quantities needed!!

Gave new meaning to the cold mirror test for employment!

FROM ROLAND SEDLUND, ADVANCED PROGRAMS GROUP

ATLAS PAYLOADS UP, UP AND AWAY, REALLY

In the 1960s and 1970s we were receiving many requests for programs which could be adapted to the Atlas F launch vehicles, which were declared surplus by the Air Force. One request which we received was from a company which saw a need for launching the ashes from deceased persons into orbit. I suggested calling this program "Up your Ashes," but the program never flew. Probably an inappropriate name?

FROM TOM LEECH

WARDROBE REVIEW TIME

During this time wardrobes made a major shift. Maybe it was "Saturday Night Fever" applied to Monday morning, but men started showing up with leisure suits, white shoes, and flashy neckwear;

women with minis and slit skirts. A new boss (a guy named Buck) arrived and didn't like what he saw. He was particularly concerned that our dress was too casual when meeting with customers. He decreed that it was time to upgrade the wardrobes back to a more conservative business look. No more of those white shoes, for example. So employees headed over to the clothing stores to get the right look. Said one colleague: "That pronouncement did more for the men's haberdashery business in San Diego than any other event."

From SPIKE WOLFENSBERGER

BUCK BUCHANAN'S RIVETING SPEECH TO DISPLACED ENGINEERS

At one time, a group of Tomahawk engineers were unceremoniously relocated to the Kearny Mesa Building Five main floor at the northeast side of the high bay area just south of the east–west aisle from the clean room and painting facility. It was noisy due to the clanging of the traveling overhead bridge cranes carrying eighty-foot long Atlas missiles. Also just west of us was the Atlas Thrust Section Assembly shop. Here, longitudinal stiffeners were riveted along the length of ten-foot diameter missile thrust sections. It was often a noisy environment and we were eventually given ear protectors. There would be a week or two with the whine of drills for rivet holes, followed by about a week of the battering noise of riveting hammers inside those thrust sections.

At about the same time, Buck Buchanan had started a "Walking Around and Talking" activity using a portable speaker-equipped podium to personally tell us, at each of our various working locations about the state of the company. We learned of his scheduled visit to our area.

One of our young engineers named Eli Kwam had made friends over in the Thrust Section assembly shop and realized with the drilling under way that riveting was due about the same time as Buck Buchanan's scheduled arrival to give his corporate speech. Eli went to his shop friends and arranged to have things relatively quiet and to wait for his wave to resume riveting.

Buchanan set up and began his talk. Eli then gave his high sign and you could no longer hear "The Talk." Many of us pulled out our ear protectors while Buchanan's lieutenants made a futile attempt to try and locate the sources of the rat-a tat-tat. Eli was our hero, but it still took ages before we were relocated.

FROM DENNY HUBER

MURPHY AT WORK AGAIN

In 1978 GD was trying to get NASA interested in integrating Centaur into the Space Shuttle, so we arranged a meeting at Johnson Space Center (JSC) in Houston, Texas. John Karas, Jim Rager, and myself were scheduled to depart San Diego one evening. After boarding our flight the pilot told us that we could not take-off due to fog. We were told we could de-plane while waiting for the weather to clear but were told to remain in the gate area. So we got off.

Without making any re-boarding announcement our flight left without us. (I assume the pilot had a brief break in the fog and didn't want to take the time to re-board those of us who had de-planed.) We were able to book a red-eye flight departing a few hours later.

When we arrived in Houston the next morning we found out that Jim's and my checked bags were waiting for us. Unfortunately John's carry-on baggage had flown on to New Orleans. We rented motel rooms so we could shower and two of us could change clothes (no time to sleep) and went on to our meeting at JSC. The meeting was not nearly as memorable as the trip getting there.

Footnote: even though the eventual Shuttle-Centaur (S/C) program was cancelled eight years later (after the Challenger failure) the program gave many of GD's engineers the opportunity to utilize and display their talent. Many of these S/C engineers (like John Karas, Jim Sponnick, Bill Johns, and Mike Jacobs to name a few) are presently leading Lockheed Martin's launch vehicle efforts.

From JACK SMOTHERS, Kearny Mesa Art and Editorial Department

Who you lookin' for?

The Art and Editorial Department at that time (in the late 70s) occupied the whole south end of Building 3. Big space, many employees—including two and only two African-American men.

One, Wendell Baker, was a street-wise paste-up guy (low man among the artist types in A&E. Not too much education). Spent the day bent over his drawing board. So no one outside A&E had reason to come see him. The other fellow, Aaron Banks, a smart college grad, was the man to see in Presentations. So he had many visitors, mostly engineers, inquiring how their projects were proceeding.

One morning a very white Anglo engineer comes into A&E for the first time. He spots Wendell, who sat just inside the door. He goes to Wendell, who, as usual, is hunched over his drawing board, and says, "Good morning. You must be Aaron Banks."

Wendell never even looks up. He simply points with his left arm into the room and casually replies, "You're looking for the other one." Instantly in his mind, Wendell could hear the engineer's boss: "Okay, go down to Art and Editorial and see the black guy." Racial profiling even at GD.

From SPIKE WOLFENSBERGER

Contract Negotiation is an art

It seemed that almost every time we went over to negotiate the costs of a contract change, Vern Boyer, our manager in Florida, who seemed to be a gifted negotiator, was able to easily justify the higher costs than the Corps of Engineers had in their plan. An example was when Vern had to justify the cost for a bunch of electrical connectors. Vern happened to have handy in his briefcase an Allied catalog listing the exact part with the cost we were claiming.

Later that same month Vern and I needed some information from our contracting officer and arrived at our appointment time to find that we would have to wait until he was done watching some sort of presentation movie in the nearby conference room nearby. The secretary said it would be a while and that it should be all right that since there was extra room in the back, we could slip in and watch also.

It turned out the movie showed how a negotiator with his estimate was to work with a contractor to get his asking cost down to agree with the government estimate. As the movie ended, Vern said "We'd better slip out of here before they realize we're here."

Our contracting officer finally emerged and waved us into his office. His first words were "OK now you've seen how it's supposed to work. What else can I do for you?" It was difficult to keep a straight face!

From TOM LEECH, Convair Marketing-Ombudsman

Proposals can present problems, or maybe not

Some will remember the RSNF proposal from the late seventies. This was GD's bid to develop the Royal Saudi Naval Facility, over on the Arabian peninsula where the Saudi naval vessels could dock and get support. Bet you didn't know GD had a background that would give us a good bidding edge (neither did I and I was given the job of writing the proposal relevant background-history). The proposal team was set up at a Lindbergh Field building for a loong project.

An important part of the process was to prepare the presentation for the customer meeting. It was well-crafted, with many visual aids key to selling our story. In our major practice session the Red Team audience included a Saudi expert. Up popped slide one, the agenda chart with the major topics placed around the map of the Arabian Peninsula. "Problem there," the Saudi expert said, "You'll lose this bid on your first slide." Huh, what's wrong with it? "You show the water area as the Persian Gulf. The Saudis' maps show that as the Arabian Gulf." Oops, guess us regular proposal types need some back-to-school geography lessons.

Some others will recall this one. For another later proposal (un-named—I was external orals coach) we were teamed with a European firm that had relevant experience for this possible contract. They had a couple of sharp people in San Diego working on the proposal. "Lars" was a key player as he had experience with a vital technology. When it came time for the proposal oral presentation to the customer, we had a team dress rehearsal, with presenters wearing wardrobe they would wear for the actual event. Lars wore a sort-of classic European outfit, a strong contrast to our typical business suits. OK, it was fun and just a rehearsal. Two days later the presentation team met the customer, and Lars was wearing that same unusual garb. Well, can't do much about that now.

Later I was able to talk with one of the members of the customer Source Evaluation Board. He said they all got a chuckle out of Lars' wardrobe choice. And about Lars' presentation? "He was excellent as he gave us important info about this critical technology and responded well to our many questions. During our later reviews of the several bidders, we concluded that whichever team won, they would have to include Lars as part of their team." What happened to that "Dress for Success" mantra? FYI, no one won the contract as the program was cancelled.

From Dick Smith

Shake, rattle and Roll!

At Lindbergh Field around 1978 or 1979, Liz Walton was Manager of Telephone Systems—one of the Administrative Services departments. She comes into my office and we have a meeting on some matter that I can't recall (not important to the story). As she gets up to leave, I say, "I got these new pills from the doctor for my blood pressure. I sure hope they can knock it down some."

So I pop the pill in my mouth and swallow. Just as I swallow, the whole building starts to shake and rumble. "Yipes!" I yell to Liz, "I'll never take those pills again!"

Liz roars as she gets under the door frame "It's an earthquake, not your pills!" Being from the East Coast it was my first earthquake experience. Those were the days my friend!!!!

CHAPTER 6—1980s TO THE PRESENT

Primary operations at General Dynamics (GD) Space Systems.

Programs included:

- Atlas and Centaur space rockets until sold to Martin
- Tomahawk Cruise Missiles (CM) and Advanced CM until sold to Hughes, then Raytheon
- Superconducting Super Collider

FROM JOHN MEDINA, PAST GD SECURITY GUARD

CATERING TO THE BOARD – NO EASY TASK

A GD Board of Directors meeting (date not recalled) was held in San Diego at the Holiday Inn at the Wharf. Ft. Worth security agents were sent out to check all rooms and the Board's Conference Room for "bugs."

TALE 1

Barbara Freeman and I were assigned to the entry of the "Peacock" Banquet Room. Barbara noticed that Colonel Henry Crown and Mrs. Crown were heading to the *hotel dining area* (coffee room). Barbara asked me to go and alert the Colonel and his wife that the breakfast was being served at the *Peacock Banquet Room*. I approached and greeted them, then showed them my GD identification (they were sipping their coffee). Mrs. Crown put her hand on mine and stated, "My dear man, the Colonel and I prefer to have our toast and coffee here. We don't want to be with those 'High Mucky-Mucks'."

I said, "Yes, Ma'am." Barbara was sort of "stunned" but we had a good chuckle.

Afterwards during the day and evening, when Mrs. Crown would be introduced to anyone, her standard greeting was "How do you do? I'm Gladys and Gladys is glad to be in San Diego." She wore a bright orange two-piece suit all three days the Board met here. Colonel Crown's routine during the three days of meetings was to go to the barber shop. On the first day he left the barber shop he then left the premises. Barbara asked me to keep an eye on him.

I followed 15 to 20 paces behind the Colonel as he carried his Homberg hat in his right hand. He started down Pacific Highway sidewalk, crossed the highway at Ash St. and back down Harbor Dr. to the hotel. All the time I'm thinking, "I'm supposed to keep an eye on the billionaire; I hope no one tries to kidnap him." I would have done my best to protect him of course. Barbara asked where I'd been. I said, "The Colonel and I took a walk!" I explained it all to her and she was amazed!

STAY TUNED FOR TALE 2

Another wife of a Board Member approached Barbara and told her she had lost a diamond-encrusted family heirloom brooch. Barbara directed her to me. The lady said they had dinner at Anthony's Fish Grotto. I first contacted hotel security, gave them the description and point of contact. The next morning I was knocking on the door of Anthony's; the staff was cleaning up. Someone came to the door and I told them I need to relay some info to the manager—to keep an eye out for the brooch and the point of contact info. That evening the lost brooch lady approached me saying, "My dear man, I'm so sorry I put you through all that searching for my brooch. We found it on the bed. When my husband put my wrap on, apparently it fell on the bed."

From JAKE (GERARD) SZATKOWSKI,
TECHNICAL PROJECT MGR.—FLIGHT DEMOS & SMALLSATS, UNITED LAUNCH ALLIANCE (ULA), DENVER

CRUISE MISSILE ACRONYM MAKES SENSE...OR DOES IT?

I was working at Kearny Mesa on the Sea Launch Cruise Missile (SLCM), Air Launch Cruise Missile (ALCM) and Ground Launch Cruise Missile (GLCM) programs in the early 1980s. We were doing advance munitions and ship identification using a superfast pattern recognition system then. Then we had the bright idea of bombing a runway with sub-munitions and that was way cool.

So they need a new name for this variant and we came up with the Full Utility Cruise Missile (FUCM). This term actually went out the door to the pentagon before anyone thought of how this sounded.

It lasted for about 5 days till it got changed.

From JIM ARNOTT, Mid-late eighties
DEPARTMENT 311-0

TEAMWORK SOMETIMES GETS TRICKY

I was the Quality Engineering member of the Lindbergh Field Numerical Control (NC) Proofing Team. The NC Proofing team had members from QC, QE, Production Control and Manufacturing Engineering. It was our task to evaluate the Inspection Report, the QA Report and the metal to determine if the numerical control tape (or later on, code) was capable of producing an acceptable part.

One morning, we were gathered at the north end of the Omni line in Lindbergh Field Building One. As we were looking things over, I realized that I didn't have a pencil. I asked Carlos, the Manufacturing Engineer, if I could borrow his.

His reply: "Do you see this pencil?" holding up a brand new, freshly sharpened gray GD pencil.

"Yes," as I reached for it.

Carlos snatched it away and said, "If I let you use my pencil, you will no doubt make an error and without thinking, will erase to correct your mistake. Then you will return the pencil to me. I will put it back in my pocket and later, when I am in a meeting, someone of importance will look and see the pencil with the used eraser in my pocket. This will lead them to erroneously conclude that I, Carlos, made a mistake. I'm sorry, I cannot allow that."

He then returned the pencil to his pocket.

From BOB EIDSON

Calendars need to pass inspection

While Chief of the Propulsion/Fluids/Mechanisms Group in the eighties (can't recall the group number but I was assigned as chief after Al Vinzant was promoted) I had a young lady engineer who became upset with the guys who had Playboy Magazine calendars displayed on their desks, with naked ladies in plain view of all. This was during the time when sexual discrimination was not as yet a sensitive issue as it is today.

I came to work one morning to discover that all those calendars had overnight been decorated with penis cutouts from a (different) magazine, scotch taped to appropriate parts of the female anatomy! The lady engineer openly claimed responsibility for the modifications which had been made.

As a result, all of those calendars disappeared from the scene and never showed up again!!!

In addition to being an excellent engineer, she was a very gutsy lady and respected by all! A couple years later, she decided to go to Israel to successfully continue her engineering career.

From MICHAEL SIMON

Nifty way to prepare for a NASA presentation Vintage Huntsville, Alabama, circa 1984.

Back in those days, we young engineers were rarely content to call it a night after dinner. We usually stayed at the Hilton across from the main concert/sports arena. One night a fellow engineer Ray Gorski and I were having drinks in the Hilton bar when we spied two attractive young gals sitting at the bar. So as any red-blooded single twenty-five year-olds would, we approached them and engaged them in light conversation. These gals were very young, probably no more than about twenty-one, if that, and were obviously fairly simple. So we were surprised when they informed us they were students at UCLA.

After we showed our surprise, they both laughed and said that in Huntsville, UCLA stood for "University of Calhoun 'Longside the Airport." Evidently it was a junior college called Calhoun College which, of course was right near the airport. We then told the gals we were in town on NASA business, to which we received quizzical expressions, forcing us to explain, "NASA, you know, the Space Program." This clearly rang a bell with the gals, who then got very excited and began asking questions about space.

When we told them we were designing vehicles to go to the Moon and Mars, they asked us, quite earnestly, if we had both been to the Moon. To which we of course told them yes, we were famous astronauts. We then ended up driving around Huntsville with them, stopping by our first "Piggly Wiggly" to buy beer and then, at the girls' suggestion, visiting what they told us was a haunted graveyard.

By this time it was well after midnight, and the girls came running out of the graveyard screaming after they apparently encountered one of the Huntsville spirits. The girls then took us to a nearby house party where we stayed up until about five or six a.m. By then all the gals had paired up with other guys and all that was left for us was a dog, so we finally left.

It was just as well because Ray and I both had to give presentations on our Orbital Transfer Vehicle project starting at eight a.m., so we had just enough time to go back to the hotel, shower, change, and then meet up with Bill Ketchum and the rest of the team as if we'd been asleep the whole night like everyone else. As usual, our presentations were well received and the trip was a huge success!

ADD-ON TO MIKE'S TALE, FROM BILL KETCHUM.

I will of course not forget when we were all in Huntsville when I turned 50. I had gone to bed early at our hotel and around midnight you and others awoke me knocking on my door and bounded in with a bottle of champagne. You guys always had something unexpected in your arsenal of tricks. These were probably the most exciting years of my career.

FROM GLEN WADLEIGH

ANOTHER INTERNATIONAL TIE—WHICH DESTINATION IS EASIER TO GET TO?

A major Design Review was to be held in Sassenheim, Netherlands. The project was an International effort between European Space Agency and NASA for the first planned mission aboard the Shuttle-Centaur. The primary GD Program officer got ill and I was offered the opportunity to represent GD.

After the formal presentations and "atta-boys", we dispersed for socializing and feasting in Amsterdam. To minimize the traffic in the roads between the infamous canals we were offered car pools. Frances and I accepted an offer to ride with the NASA Principal Payload Astronaut and his wife. They were wonderful company but

I felt obliged to chide him about heading to space but getting lost on his way to the restaurant.

FROM CONNIE TERWILLIGER, TV/MOTION PICTURE DEPARTMENT, KEARNY MESA (THE HIDDEN FILM FACTORY)

FIRST OFF—CHECK OUT THE PLACE(S)

My first day on the job at GD Convair was a Monday in February, 1986. I spent it in the air flying to Electric Boat in Groton, Connecticut. They had allowed me to pick up my badge the previous Friday at the front desk, but since I wasn't really on the job yet, I didn't get to go down to the Film and Video Department in Building Four that day. I had been hired as a producer/writer/talent and my boss Scott Crist and I were on an initial location scout for a corporate piece.

February in Groton is cold. I was unprepared. The PR guy loaned me a boot length fur-lined man's coat in order to keep me warm during our tour of the submarine plant. His main concern was that it was getting close to lunch time and he didn't want me—a female—to be in the "yard" when the flood of workers exited the plant to drink their lunch at the row of bars across the street from the plant.

I was bundled up so completely, that the only possible way that anyone could tell I was female was by the red boots I was wearing. I escaped un-harmed. The submarine plant was awesome.

We headed off to St. Louis for a day or two of meetings before continuing on to Ft. Worth and the F-16. Again, what can I say but awesome. And I had time after touring the mile-long plant and watching a test flight of a brand new jet to go boot shopping.

Next stop, Abilene, to visit a plant that ground out cruise missile bodies and dunked them in some sort of caustic chemicals in order to make them strong. OK, I'm an actor, not an engineer. I'm sure someone knows what actually happened there in Abilene, but this was near the end of a whirlwind trip and I was getting a bit shell-shocked. In fact, while being shown the dark room, we went through one of those little black out chambers and I blacked out.

The next Monday, I met my boss at the Kearny Mesa Convair campus and again, bypassing my office, we drove up to Pomona to see their fine selection of rockets and things. Ram, Standard, Stinger, Phalanx.

A couple of days later, I finally saw my cubicle and met some of the team I would be with for the next 8 years or so. Before they shut the doors in 1994, I had been moved to Space Systems from Convair and sold to Martin Marietta, ultimately turning in my badge to Lockheed Martin.

Over those years, not only did I get to every corner of the San Diego facilities, I got to see the tank plants in Lima, Ohio and Detroit—also awesome. The Atlas and Centaur rockets at Cape Canaveral and Vandenberg. Air Launched Cruise Missiles hanging from a B-52 at Edwards Air Force Base while trying to look pretty on the 120 degree tarmac while doing a short on-camera introduction for a classified video. I saw launch vehicle nose cones in Harlingen, Texas along with the largest cockroach that ever existed. Cessna Citations in Kansas—where blue laws prevented me from taking a drink to my hotel room from the bar. And enormous magnets in Hammond, Louisiana—where I first saw Nutria—what a waitress told me they make "fake" fur from.

It was an amazing place to work in the late eighties to mid-nineties.

Note: Connie is now a full-time voice talent working out of her professional home studio for corporate and commercial clients around the globe. Listen to her demos at voiceover-talent.com/.

From LOLA SPENCER THOMPSON, Engineering Planner (scheduling), Kennedy Space Center, from 1989 to 2005 at Launch Complex-36 and LC-4. Now at Huntsville, Alabama

Weird players down there at those launch sites.

Starting in 1989, I worked for GD at ETR (Eastern Test Range) Complex 36. Once we were GD, Martin Marietta and Lockheed Martin(LM) all in one year. Meant three W-2 forms and one desk, like that internet joke about aerospace workers. Quite a few of us are up here in Huntsville, AL now, at various places: LM, Pratt & Whitney, United Launch Alliance and more.

We try to have Cape get-togethers every couple of months and have come up with the enclosed nicknames (see a few below) and phrases used a lot from those years (1990s). If you don't already have it you should get Bob Reynolds launch history sheet (Bob: please send that). Very impressive! Look forward to your book!

TOM LEECH

PEEWEE HERMAN - JIM RAVITZ

PINKIE (ALMOST RED) - KELLES VENERI

TWINS - HARRY ARMER AND DAN SCHMIDT

BIG FELLA - BOB FOSTER

SAM - SMART ASS MAGGIE

CARL DETROIT WATSON

DOWNTOWN HOWARD BROWN

STICK BOY - RODNEY DAVIGNON

PRECIOUS - BRIDGET GRIFFIN

DRAG ASS - JOHN DRAGASH

DINGLEBERRY - BRAD BERRY

MRS. DINGLEBERRY - EUGENIA BERRY

MR. MAGOO - KEVIN ATWOOD

DEAD WOOD - GIL WOOD

MR. GREENJEANS - MIKE KENNEDY

TT - TOM THOMPSON

MONKEY - TOM CORBIN

DINK - GENE HAWN

HUMVEE - VICKIE MCLOUGHLIN

HORNY BILL - BILL HORNIG

WALKIE TALKIE WOOD - GIL WOOD

SOME MORE FASCINATING MEMORIES FROM DOWN THERE AT THE CAPE

Here are some hints about the tales, which are likely to tweak some memories from her Cape colleagues:

162

- DE Smith's wife put him on a diet but every time he opened his lunchbox there was a Twinkie sitting on top. (Now that's a tale well-tied to current events—recent headline "TWINKIES LIKELY TO SURVIVE")
- Blockhouse monitor paged the Stand Engineer—Stan Thomas called back and said 'this is Stan the Engineer'
- Captain Ike coated his bike with zinc but somehow it still rusted—any idea how that happened Kim Johnson?
- Joe Fust riding his bike to A pad and, not seeing the road roped off, did a flip (chalk outline marked the spot)
- Rob Daus going to Van Gundy's Halloween party and getting his Caddy stuck in the yard
- Mark Brown going on a blind date who ends up being Renee Page (hmm...)
- Taco Bell dog leaving messages on Jim Burke's answering machine
- Smiley face drawn on back of Kevin Wyckoff's head when it was sticking outside the thrust section
- Moving Pete Ejarque's car with fork lift
- John Martin's company car with a periscope on top (after John's son sank his personal car at the boat ramp by Grill's Seafood)
- Dick Sweatt's Atlas Launch Cake (passed on recipe to Jean Hook when he retired)

Should anyone like to amplify on these or other Cape tales, send them along.

FROM MICHAEL SIMON

TALE OF MOUSE AND MEN

Lots of stories about the old days at Kearny Mesa Building Twenty-six. I was a Senior Cost Development Engineer in the Economic Analysis group whose chief was Dwight Little, and Bob Bradley was my immediate supervisor, the lead person in our group at Kearny Mesa.

A bunch of young engineers were hired right out of school between 1979 and 1984 to work on Shuttle-Centaur as well as the expanding cruise missile program. There wasn't much hiring in the late sixties and seventies due to the aerospace downturn, so there was a big generation gap between us new hires and the in-place engineers and managers, many of whom were hired in the fifties or even the forties. I remember one guy who worked in Proposal Development who had been at GD since before Pearl Harbor.

Bill Ketchum got the honor of trying to manage programs staffed mainly by all the new hires, and the list of wild and crazy stories goes on and on. A lot of us young engineers were crammed into cubicles in the far northwest corner of Building Twenty-six to support advanced space programs, where the senior managers for Convair's Advanced Space Programs were based at the time—our Vice-President Bill Rector and his directors Don Charhut (Advanced Programs) and Doug Hayden (marketing). Key managers included Bill Strobl, Otto Steinbronn, Paul Bialla, and of course Bill. The sheer density of energetic young engineers, all crammed into such a small space, resulted in a very dynamic environment.

One time a mouse got loose in our area and it created sheer bedlam. I found a way to catch the mouse with my hands and while I was showing it off, it bit my hand and I reflexively jerked my hand violently and the mouse went flying. I ran after it and then dove to the carpet to catch it, only to realize I had just dived into Bill Strobl's office—while he was in a meeting with several Air Force colonels!

Comment from Bill Ketchum: How could I ever forget? As Tom Kessler once said "Ketchum's Kindergarten." It was like that sometimes, but more like herding cats, very intelligent, but playful.

A SHERIFF ONBOARD CONVAIR?

Many other stories relating to the old days at Kearny Mesa Building Twenty-six. Perhaps the most infamous of all the episodes was the "Sheriff Bill Ketchum" drama. Somebody, I'll never say who, took a piece of chalk and, while Bill was momentarily away from his office, drew a Happy Face (J) on the fabric cushion on Bill's office chair. It seemed like an innocent enough prank at the time, but for some reason, even though Bill had been very tolerant of many other misdeeds, this particular incident really pissed him off.

For some reason Bill suspected innocent little me of drawing the happy face, so he came over to my cubicle and said, in the whiney nasal voice he sometimes used when he got angry, "Simon, I know you did it. Why don't you confess?" To which I claimed I had no knowledge of what Bill was talking about. At some point, Bill got so angry he actually kicked my chair.

Keep in mind this all happened in plain view of about twenty young engineers, none over the age of twenty-five, and all of whom could barely constrain their laughter. Soon after, "WANTED" posters appeared throughout Building Twenty-six, with a photo of Bill taken from one of our proposals, crudely modified to show him wearing a Sheriff's hat and badge, and showing the Happy Face as the fugitive. Like any good WANTED poster, it showed the front and side facial views of the villain.

BILL KETCHUM

ATLAS GETTING RUSSIAN ENGINES??

My last job at GD was working with the Russians to install their engines in the Atlas. The first meeting was here in San Diego with their senior engineer, a younger guy, and the most beautiful young female I have ever seen. You can imagine how that first meeting went.

On arrival a GD Human Resources person escorted the Russians into the meeting room. The older Russian engineer introduced himself, Felix Chelkis. The very young Russian said nothing, didn't join us at the table and sat behind us just listening which made me conclude that he was a KGB agent taking note of everything I said.

After chatting for a few minutes with the older Russian engineer in perfect English, the door opened and in walked a very beautiful young female white Russian, creamy white complexion, and joined us at the table whereupon the old Russian engineer introduced her as his junior engineer.

I was stunned just looking at her and as the discussion followed I found myself unable to formulate my thoughts or words out of my mouth and I must have sounded like an idiot.

She was very knowledgeable and rattled off technical information on their rocket engines and how they might be adapted to our Atlas rocket. To this day I can't remember anything I might have said.

Several more meetings over the next few months concluded with a dinner at a restaurant along San Diego Bay directly across from Naval Air Station, North Island where several of our aircraft carriers were docked, which seemed of great interest to the Russians, especially the KGB agent.

After dinner, and a round of vodka of course, the older Russian engineer presented me with a very nice decorated wooden soup spoon saying that it was customary in Russian culture for comrades to eat soup from the same bowl as a gesture of comradeship.

I have this spoon to this day and value it highly

FUN ON THE JOB

FROM LEROY GROSS HEAD RICKETY ROCKETEER

DOING OUR JOB—GETTING THEM UP THERE

The countdowns at the Cape were long and sometimes boring, so I would sit at my console and write poetry. Here is one I wrote while we were launching a spy satellite:

Sometimes I sit here and wonder why
We shoot our missiles into the sky.
They work all right
And get out of sight
But Security here is so very tight
That we've never learned if the Spacecraft burned
Its engines and got to where it should be
Or if its sensors failed to spy
On imaginary enemies from way up high.
Perhaps someday when we're old and gray
The history books will quietly say
That the CIA was here today.

OTHER RELATED BOOKS

Atlas 50th Reunion Committee, 1957-2007: *Celebrating 50 Years of Atlas Success & the People Who Made It Possible*

Bill Chana, *Over the Wing: the Bill Chana Story*

Convair Aerospace Division of General Dynamics/Fiftieth Anniversary 1923-1973

Chuck DeMund, *My Accidental Life*

Roger Franklin, *The Defender: The Story of General Dynamics*

GD Convair Division, A Convair History, 1989 Desk Calendar

General Dynamics Convair Division 1989, *Liberator: Consolidated Vultee. The Need, The Plane, The Crew, The Missions*

Jacob Goodwin, *Brotherhood of Arms: General Dynamics and the Business of Defending America*

Ed Hujsak, *A Pig in the Rumble Seat and other short stories*

John Chapman, *Atlas: the Story of a Missile*, Harper NY 1960

Lily Koppel, *The Astronaut Wives Club*

Ted Lamoureux, *My Life at Convair*

Mercury Astronauts, *We Seven: By the Astronauts Themselves*

NASA, *Project Mercury: A Chronology*

NASA History Office (CD-ROM), *The Centaur Upper Stage Rocket: Taming Liquid Hydrogen*

San Diego County Television Network (DVD 2007), "50 years of Atlas"

Jack Smothers and Roy Gjertson, *Convair Aerospace Division of General Dynamics 50th Anniversary 1923-1973*

Convair division of GD Space 1959, *Primer: An Introduction to Astronautics*

United Launch Alliance (DVD): "Atlas, Fifty Years and Counting 1957-2007

William Wagner, *Reuben Fleet, and the Story of Consolidated Aircraft*

Chuck Walker, *Atlas, the Ultimate Weapon*

Bob Ward, *The Light Stuff: Space Humor – From Sputnik to Shuttle*

Tom Wolfe, *The Right Stuff*

Bill Yenne, *Into the Sunset: The Convair Story*

INDEX

READER'S NOTES

BOOK ORDERING
INFORMATION

For copies of *Fun on the Job*, you can get them at amazon.com and presentationspress.com. Also at some bookstores.

ABOUT TOM LEECH

Tom Leech was with the San Diego General Dynamics aerospace operation for two decades, with assignments in business development, engineering and internal communication (including as division ombudsman, one of the first in corporate America). That GD career provided a solid base for starting his own consulting firm as a presentations coach, seminar leader and conference speaker.

Photo by Gertraud Strangl

His articles have appeared in many publications, including *San Diego Magazine*, *Presentations*, *Frontier Airlines*, *Executive Excellence*, and *The Toastmaster*. His article "How General Dynamics Integrated the Cape," originally in the *San Diego Union*, was reprinted in *Quest: the History of Spaceflight Quarterly*.

The third edition of his highly-successful book, *How To Prepare, Stage & Deliver Winning Presentations* (AMACOM, 2004), was lauded as one of only two "Top of the Class" books on the subject by Presentations Magazine. He's author of *Say it like Shakespeare: the Bard's Timeless Tips for Communication Success,* an update of the McGraw-Hill First Edition, which has received high praise from many quarters.

Wearing his weekend hat he is co-author, with GD colleague Jack Farnan, of *Outdoors San Diego: Hiking, Biking and Camping* (Premier 2004) and was longtime Editor of the Outdoors Forum for *San Diego Magazine*. With his traveler's hat, he describes his six-months' wandering the world in *On the Road in '68: a year of turmoil, a journey of friendship.* Donning his poet's cap, he and wife

Leslie Johnson-Leech are authors of the children's tale *The Curious Adventures of Santa's Wayward Elves*.

For information about all of his books, visit presentationspress.com. For information about Tom's coaching, training and speaking services, visit winning-presentations.com. And to expand your nature enjoyment, visit outdoorssandiego.com.